RETIREMENT RADICALS

A Design Handbook for the Boomer Generation
to be Post-Career World-Changers

DAVE WITMER

Retirement Radicals
A Design Handbook for the Boomer Generation to be Post-Career World-Changers
by Dave Witmer

Printed in the United States of America

ISBN 9781498423878

www.xulonpress.com

Contents

Acknowledgements

I am grateful to the HopeNet Fellowship of Churches with whom I serve for graciously providing a summer sabbatical break. This time away allowed me to craft a book from ideas that I had been pondering for some time. A big thanks goes to my always emotionally and spiritually supportive wife, Carol, and to Kathy Campbell; both invested hours checking and rechecking the text.

I appreciated conversations with leaders and friends that provided personal insights into the hopes and dreams of individuals. I also find the Bible to be full of interesting, very human characters finding their way on a journey through life. There is nothing like a good story, and the Scriptures have more than a few. And so Biblical texts are woven throughout this book.

Among the many "gods" people might seek, my inspiration comes from the God Scripture describes as the "Living God." I use this term in the book intentionally to honor Someone not made of stone, not merely a philosophy, a metaphor, a force field or an earth-energy. The Living God is so much more full and dynamically personal than any of these. If you have not yet met the Living God, I hope you do so quite soon, for this God gives meaning to any season of life.

Introduction

*T*he fact that you are reading this suggests that aging and possible retirement might be on your mind. You are not alone!

A demographic transformation is underway in America, one that has been growing slowly over the last century. Starting in 2011, the first of the 79 million member Baby Boomer generation, those born between 1946 and 1964, turned age 65. Comprising 26% of the total U.S. population this massive wave of adults is growing at a rate of 10,000 per day. It's been described as the "pig moving through the python." An unflattering metaphor, but we get the vivid picture.

It is no accident that God has allowed this enormous amount of older adults to be alive at this time in history. This aging Boomer cohort has great promise of significant accomplishments for God's mission. God is up to something good in His worldwide redemptive purposes.

> *It is no accident that God has allowed this enormous amount of older adults to be alive at this time in history.*

Will Boomers continue to change the world in their older "retirement" years? Will churches, faith communities and service organizations mobilize them?

Needed: A Practical Handbook

As I collected materials related to the aging Boomer future I found well-written books urging that something should be, and must be, done to anticipate this new retirement generation. But what seemed missing from the book list were resources that would help a leader or a Boomer actually think and plan for his or her future. Many books provided a well-defined "wake-up call" but stopped short of offering a pastor or a 60 year-old what to do once he or she was awake. So, I set out to design a practical handbook, and my hope is that at least two groups of people benefit from using it.

If You are a Leader

First, this study is for pastors and leaders who are looking for resources to mobilize the tremendous potential of the aging Boomers in their congregations and their communities. This active older population group will only increase in number, and the wise leader will be proactive in seeking what God has in store for this work force.

Many Boomers resist the prospect of retiring. They cringe at the term "senior citizen" – coined in the 1930s – and are replacing it with new vocabulary. For example, Pensacola Covenant Church in Redwood City, California uses the term "Plus Ministries," emphasizing that older adults have something to add to people's lives. Recently I heard a leader refer to "Seasoned" Citizens. Call it retirement, or post-career *un-retirement,* reality is catching up with Boomers, and life will change.

I hope pastors and leaders sense the urgency and opportunity before them as millions of Americans turn 65. Some leaders will need a wake-up call to the needs and potentials of the "new old" with whom they minister. Others already see the breeze picking up and want to be ready to set sail. The call is not to reshape the church merely to serve the demands of this generation, but to harness the tremendous potential for meaningful service. 79 million Boomers are looking for something more than shuffleboard tournaments.

To paraphrase an old Zig Ziglar proverb, "The only thing worse than empowering people and then losing them, is not to empower them and keep them." In his book, *Prime Time*, Marc Freedman states, "Older Americans may well be our only *increasing* natural resource." He adds, "America's burgeoning older population is poised to become the new trustees of civic life in the country."[1]

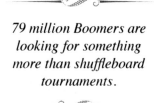

79 million Boomers are looking for something more than shuffleboard tournaments.

Ambassador James Joseph, of Duke's Sanford School of Public Policy, addressed the First International Conference on Age-Friendly Cities with this challenge, "While medical science in the last century has succeeded in extending the human life by twenty years, our policies, practices and perceptions have not changed. It is not that we have failed to ascribe a legitimate social function to the added twenty years; we have not taken advantage of the emotional wisdom and social intellegence available to a world desperately in need of leaders with the moral and spiritual intellegence they bring."[2]

If you are a pastor or leader who finds older adult ministry intimidating, it's time to rethink your perceptions. 65 year-old Boomers will be dramatically unlike any previous senior generation you may have seen or served. As a young pastor I enjoyed interacting with older adults, but dreaded the scowls of a few bitter souls and their grumpy tirades against "the young generation." But lay those dismal images of the elderly aside; aging Boomers look at the world very differently than their parents. We'll explore characteristics of the "new old" in **Part I**.

If You are a Boomer

The second primary reader to benefit is the Boomer, who, like myself, is looking ahead to that altered post-career "radical retirement" season of life. Some of us will be able to plan ahead carefully with plenty of time to spare. Others will not have that luxury. Corporate downsizing, heath changes or other circumstances might surprise us with sudden transition away from one's full-time career. If that is your situation, take heart. Many retirees discover new significance after their retirement period has already begun because they can rest and have time to stop and refocus.

In 1971, Alvin Lee and his blues-rock band Ten Years After sang their hit single "I'd Love to Change the World (but I don't know what to do)." The song summarized the confusion many young Boomers felt about the violent and confusing 1960s. Would the new decade of the 1970s be different? Now decades later, adult Boomers may not have the same bewildered longing about the future, but each season of life echoes the same question, "I'd love to change the world, but I don't know what to do." My desire is that this book provides practical ways for you to reflect and engage in a meaningful and fulfilling post-career season of life. Many Boomers, and one could argue, *most* Boomers, want to make a difference, and so, with a few adjustments, the dreaded "retirement age" zone can become one of the most impactful segments on one's entire life.

Some Boomers will make a post-career transition early at age 62, others will target age 70. Some of us will reduce work to remain employed part-time within a professional career field, while others will readjust to a smaller consultant role when needed, or will assist in research and development. Others will leave all employment within a former career field and will become active volunteers.

Peter Drucker once said, "The best way to predict the future is to create it." If you are a Boomer anticipating retirement in the next decade, now would be a great time to create your future, to prayerfully chart a course for your post-career years.

Part II of this book is designed to be a practical handbook with reflection questions that will help you shape your future as you ease toward retirement. You'll need an old fashioned pencil and paper or your touch screen electronic device. You will be invited to take stock of your personal assets in eight areas:

My calling – What is my unique life purpose?
My skills – What can I do?
My stuff – What do I own?
My insight – What do I know?
My initiative – When do I lead?
My creativity – What can I make?
My schedule – How much time do I have?

Serving with Integrity

Retirement requires transition and realignment of position, authority, status, and responsibility, and **Part III** will focus on how to gracefully reposition yourself under the authority of others so that you add tremendous value to your church and local community.

Putting This Book to Work

In summary, this book is designed to be a practical handbook for leaders and for those anticipating a transition to post-career retirement. It can easily be used as a personal study, however, reflecting together on each chapter with a group can enrich your insight. Boomers love to hear others' stories, and talking about your future with others can strengthen your personal discovery. Group conversation positions you to support each other as you pursue the ventures to which God might be calling you.

Group contexts might include:

A small group study. Share your journey with 6-10 people in a Bible Study group, home fellowship, or a lunch group.

A Sunday educational class. If your church has Sunday morning Christian education classes for adults, use this book for a 13-week elective quarter.

Pastoral post-career counseling. Pastors or other counselors may find the reflection questions helpful for mentoring and coaching sessions.

A weekend retreat. Sometimes a concentrated focus in a relaxed setting can provide a memorable milestone of spiritual insight. A weekend away might be organized for Boomers who are preparing for retirement with the potential to leave the retreat event with fresh excitement about the futre.

A community workshop or seminar series. Some congregations provide midweek classes or workshops that serve not only their members but also the broader community. Inviting community neighbors to your local congregation might introduce Boomers, especially those who do not participate in a faith community, to how meaningful and relevant the local church is to navigate real life issues.

Part I – The Boomer Journey

Do not use
your new *post-career* freedom as an excuse
to do anything you want.

Use it
as an opportunity
to serve each other with love.

— adapted from Galatians 5:13

CHAPTER ONE

The Boomer Demographic Bulge

*L*et's start with a brief overview of the "Boomer" generation. Following World War II, thousands of soldiers returned home and sought to restart their lives as civilians. Many women who had served in the military or worked outside of the home in the absence of their husbands also adjusted to new post-war routines in marriage and family life. For many, this meant starting a family that had been delayed by the war.

Up until 1946 births per year in the United States were less than 3 million. But from 1946 through 1964 the birthrate skyrocketed, it *boomed*, and the term stuck! Between 1946 and 1954 births jumped to 3.5 million per year, and between 1955 and 1964 babies were arriving at a rate of 4.2 million per year.

New schools had to be built. Farm and ranch lands were transformed into vast seas of "cookie-cutter' suburban housing developments. America teemed with children. Similar increased birth rates occurred in Canada where six million are known as "boomies." In Britain this post-war generation is known as "the bulge."

The Boomer generation can be further identified in two broadly defined groups: **Leading-Edge** Baby Boomers were born between 1946 and 1955. These individuals came of age during the Vietnam War era. The second group, called Late

Boomers, or **Trailing-Edge** Boomers, was born between 1956 and 1964. They do not remember JFK's Camelot, but do remember Nixon's Watergate.

Boomers and the American Dream

Preceding the Second World War Americans had endured the great Depression and the Dust Bowl. Boomers' parents were a generation hardened by poverty. Millions had been deprived of the security of a home and job. Now a strong post-war economy led couples to expand their families.

In his 1931 book *Epic of America* Historian James Truslow Adams first popularized the "American Dream," a vision that began to take root in the post-war Boomer generation. Adams wrote,

> "But there has been also the *American dream*, that dream of a land in which life should be better and richer and fuller for every man, with opportunity for each according to his ability or achievement... It has been a dream of being able to grow to fullest development as a man and woman, unhampered by the barriers which had slowly been erected in the older civilizations, unrepressed by social orders which had developed for the benefit of classes rather than for the simple human being of any and every class."[1]

Many Boomers embraced Adam's notion of richness and fullness, having it all while not being encumbered by the "barriers of the older generation." A heady idealism about new ideas and freedom of expression swept Boomers' teenage expectations. But visions of a world of peace, love and harmony clashed with harsh realities of the bloody war in Vietnam and the up-hill struggle for racial civil rights. The American dream was still a nightmare for many.

Leading Edge Boomers were terrified of polio, and Trailing Edge Boomers feared "the bomb." The Boomers were the first of any human generation to be reared under the real threat of total annihilation through thermonuclear war. New "super power" nations bristled with weapons of mass destruction. During the 1947-1991 Cold War Era when the U.S. faced off with the former Soviet Union, young Boomers were taught in school to "duck and cover" when air-raid sirens sounded in preparation for the searing flash of a Soviet nuclear blast. Thousands of years of human existence could be snuffed out in the blinding flashes of a global thermonuclear exchange. And as thousands of young soldiers died in the jungles of Vietnam Boomer teens and college students sensed a new urgency for world peace. "Make love, not war!" became a philosophy of life for young Boomers.

Despite these aspirations for a communally shared peace and utopia a powerful new self-centered consumer culture also emerged. The American Dream promised more than the absence of the horrors of foreign wars and a nuclear firestorm, it also promised riches – a life of personal convenience and pleasure.

Many of us Boomers grew up in the 1950-70s with an abundance of material goods that our parents had not known.

Following World War II, production of non-military household, recreational and luxury items resumed. Many of us Boomers grew up in the 1950-70s with an abundance of material goods that our parents had not known.

Malls, Credit Cards, TV and IRAs

On October 8, 1956, some 40,000 visitors swarmed to the grand opening of a new type of shopping experience in Edina, Minnesota. Southdale Center became the first indoor, multi-store shopping center in the US. The center creators saw that consumers increasingly demanded both convenience and variety, and as a result, this shopping hub placed 72 stores under one roof. The *mall* was born.

In September 1958, the BankAmericard became the first successful modern credit card, eventually evolving into the Visa system. In 1966, a group of banks established Master Charge to compete with BankAmericard. Early credit cards were mass-produced and mass-mailed unsolicited to bank customers. A card in your name simply showed up in your mailbox one day. This practice created significant financial chaos and was outlawed in 1970, but not until 100 million credit cards had been dropped into the young U.S. Boomer population.

Bell Telephone Labs and AT&T introduced the first public U.S television demonstration on April 7, 1927. Pictures and sound of a speech by Herbert Hoover were sent by wire from Washington, D.C. to New York City to a 2x3 inch screen — about the size of a small smart phone. By 1966, NBC was broadcasting all its programs in "living" color.

Post-war television was still new in America west of Chicago, but its explosive expansion during the Boomer's childhood changed America's home life. By the 1980s there was at least one television in 98 percent of American homes. Boomers were the first generation to be raised on TV. Cartoons, sitcoms, movies, nightly newscasts flooded into homes. While Leading Edge Boomers do not remember a childhood with TV like Trailing Edge Boomers (1954 was the first year a majority of households had a TV), audiovisual media became as common an appliance as the kitchen stove.

In addition to entertainment and news outlets, TV was a new gold mine for consumer product promotion. Smiling door-to-door sales hawksters came from the doorstep into millions of living rooms to compel us to buy the latest, great gadget – down at the mall with a credit card! Ads became big business, selling everything from soap and cars to cigarettes and whiskey. Advertising soared from 171 million dollars in 1950 to more than 3.6 billion in 1970.[2] These consumer innovations during the Boomer generation's formative years increased discontentment and a search for the best new inventions.

Boomers were making money, and in some cases, lots of it. Studies suggest that Boomer incomes are as much as 53% above their parents earnings.[3] While Dad may have looked to Social Security and possibly a modest company pension to get him through retirement, Boomers have been funding an array of diverse post-career options, including 401(k)s, 403(b)s Traditional IRAs, Roth IRAs, SEP IRAs, Simple IRAs, Self-Directed IRAs, and Rollover IRAs.

An Educated Generation

In 1950 three-fourths of Americans over age 55 did not have a high school diploma. In contrast, today's older Boomers are well traveled and more highly educated than both their parent's generation. Among the oldest baby boomers, 87 percent are high school graduates, more than one in four have college degrees, and more than half have some college experience.[4]

And, Boomer's are more educated than their own children's generation. According to a report on the state of US education from the Council on Foreign Relations, young Americans going into the labor force today are less educated than the Boomers retiring from it. For 55-64 year-old Boomers, the U.S. has the highest percentage of high-school graduates in the world and the third-highest percentage of college graduates. But among ages 25-34, the U.S. drops to 10th in high school graduates and 13th for college graduates.[5] This trend — an older generation outpacing the education of the emerging younger generation — is unique to the U.S. among developed countries.

Cultural Shapers

Following the restrictions and rationing of the World War II years, Boomers experienced a giddy freedom to experiment with music, new forms of techno entertainment (megawattage rock concerts), psychedelic drugs (pot, LSD, cocaine, etc.), uninhibited sexuality (Playboy was launched in 1953 with a $1,000 loan from Hugh Hefner's mother), and non-Judeo-Christian worldviews.

Boomers devised new forms of religious expression both inside the Christian faith and beyond it. Boomer youth in the Jesus People movement of the early 1970s shed the pipe organ for Fender Stratocasters and drums. Recently after a contempoary worship service a sixtyish year-old Boomer lauded the young guitarist for his lightning fast licks on his Les Paul guitar. "He can play Bohemian Rhapsody like nobody," Dale raved. Boomers grew up on drums and amplifiers; there will not likely be dinner-music organ reveries in Boomer populated retirement communities.

Boomers devised new forms of religious expression both inside the Christian faith and beyond it.

Departing from the Judeo-Christian worldview that dominated American culture since colonial days, Boomers dabbled in non-Anglo eastern religions. John Lennon and the Beatles suddenly looked sexy sitting with the Maharishi Yogi in a cross-legged lotus position.

Theologians scrambled to define and warn against "cults," and the church faced a new competitive world of religious pluralism. Boomers moved from the "no god" scientific optimism of their parents to a "which god?" palette of mystical spiritual choices. Boomers saw prayer to the Judeo-Christian Almighty God excluded from its long-held place in the formal routine of the public school life. And the Boomer generation saw the legalization of abortion and the sanction of same gender marriage.

Now Boomers find themselves in a post-Christian American culture, one where the Christian story is no longer shared within society and Christianity's values and instructions no longer guide people's lives. Dr. Stuart Murray describes the current spiritual context of "post-Christendom" America with the following list of religious mindset transitions.[6]

From the center to margins: in Christendom the Christian story and the churches were central, but in post-Christendom these are marginal.

From majority to minority: in Christendom Christians comprised the (often overwhelming) majority, but in post-Christendom we are a minority.

From settlers to sojourners: in Christendom Christians felt at home in a culture shaped by their story, but in post-Christendom we are aliens, exiles and pilgrims in a culture where we no longer feel at home.

From privilege to plurality: in Christendom Christians enjoyed many privileges, but in post-Christendom we are one community among many in a plural society.

From control to witness: in Christendom churches could exert control over society, but in post-Christendom we exercise influence only through witnessing to our story and its implications.

From maintenance to mission: in Christendom the emphasis was on maintaining a supposedly Christian status quo, but in post-Christendom it is on mission within a contested environment.

From institution to movement: in Christendom churches operated mainly in institutional mode, but in post-Christendom we must become again a Christian movement.

Now the Aging Mainstream

By the close of twentieth century the Baby Boom generation had became the mainstream of American society and its leadership. U.S presidents have been Boomers beginning with Bill Clinton. Many Boomers hold sway in Congress and lower court judiciaries, and serve as CEOs of Fortune 1,000 companies. Boomers fill university professor chairs. Now that Boomers are the aging mainstream, the bravo and idealism of their teen years is tested against the realities of standing at the helm of actual governing.

In 1965, at the end of the Baby Boom, 36 percent of Americans were under the age of 18. By 2013 only 18 percent of the U.S. population was under the age of 18.[7]

U.S population under 18	1965	2013
	36%	18%

In 1935 the over-65 group accounted for 6.5 million–about 5 percent of the U.S. population. By 2030 that will have ballooned to 75 million; or 18% of the U.S. population.[8]

	1935	2030
Over-65 population	6.5 million	75 million
Percentage of U.S. population	5%	18%

To review the Boomer population demographic for your county from 2010 U.S. census data go to: http://www.governing.com/gov-data/baby-boomers-county-population-map.html

If you are a Boomer, like me, this census data simply assures us that our massive aging generation will be a significant part of American life for years to come. The force of the Boomer's life and times will continue to shape American culture. In the next chapter we'll explore how Boomers will approach their post-career life, their un-retirement.

POST-CAREER DESIGN QUESTIONS

For the Pastor – Who are your aging Boomers?

If you are a pastor or a leadership team, take a look at your faith community's demographics. Prepare a brief report about the impact of the Boomer generation's presence among you.

- How many Boomers currently participate in your worship, congregational life and ministry?
- How many are nearing age 65?
- How many are retiring or scaling back in their occupations and careers?
- What impact has Boomer-led culture had on the shape of your church life?

For the Boomer – What has shaped your view of life?

If you are a Boomer, what significant moments in the past five to six decades have shaped your view of life? Add formative events from your life that occurred during this time. Tell stories in your small group.

The 1950s

Major Events: the Korean War, first organ transplant, hydrogen bomb created, school segregation ended, Elvis, first space satellite launched.

What spiritual, educational, relational or personal milestones did you experience during the 50s?

The 1960s
Major Events: the Civil Rights Movement, color television, the Cuban Missile Crisis, JFK assassination, Vietnam War, the Beatles, MLK and RFK assassinations, the Moon landing, Woodstock.

What spiritual, educational, relational or personal milestones did you experience during the 60s?

The 1970s
Major Events: Jesus People Movement, Non-Christian religious cults, Watergate, Cambodian genocide, VCR, Iran hostages.

What spiritual, educational, relational or personal milestones did you experience during the 70s?

The 1980s
Major Events: the personal computer, AIDS identified, Chernobyl nuclear disaster, first women in space and on Supreme Court, Berlin Wall removed.

What spiritual, educational, relational or personal milestones did you experience during the 80s?

The 1990s

Major Events: Soviet Union collapses, Apartheid ends, Desert Storm, the Internet, Oklahoma City bombing, Princess Diana's death, impeachment hearings.

What spiritual, educational, relational or personal milestones did you experience during the 90s?

The 2000s

Major Events: 9/11 Terrorist Attacks, Afghan War, Iraq War, Hurricane Katrina, recession, first black president.

What spiritual, educational, relational or personal milestones did you experience during this decade?

CHAPTER TWO

The New Look of Boomer Retirement

*T*he biggest year of the U.S. birth boom was 1957, the year I was born, with 4.3 million births. Now, nearly 60 years later I'm sipping Jamaican coffee and reflecting on the exciting journey that lies ahead. There are uncertainties, to be sure. But what I do know is that my approaching post-career life (retirement) will look very different from what was typical in the generation that preceded me.

Today's grandkids will go to hear grandpa's rock band. They will watch grandma finish a marathon race. Bingo games will be replaced by a Beatles Bash. And instead of a permanent vacation, many will continue active employment at some level. Former *NBC Nightly News* Anchor Tom Brokaw continued part-time reporting after retiring from daily news cast production declaring that he would do "fewer things, slower." Aging Baby Boomers are redefining retirement, which is why the word "retirement" no longer seems to be the right term for what Boomers expect to experience.

Rethinking Church Senior Ministries

Twenty years ago "senior" ministry included regular events, such as card games, reunions or day trips to gardens, parks and museums. Builders enjoyed travelogue slide shows from fellow seniors. Maybe a peer would lecture or reminisce on a topic, and pre-Boomer "Builders" were loyal and compliant listeners.

Newly retiring Boomers much prefer activities that have a purpose, that promote a cause or that enhance wellness.

These activities are not wrong; they simply are not what Boomers look forward to. Newly retiring Boomers much prefer activities that have a purpose, that promote a cause or that enhance wellness. Boomers prefer tagging along with younger generations on mission trips or going along to their concerts. Most Boomers would rather have a class on the latest in tech innovation than go to a reunion to reminisce about yesteryear.

Bill Ness states in his article, *It's Not Your Grandma's Retirement – A Look at the Evolution of Retirement Trends*, "When it comes to retirement, that means a lifestyle that has come a long way from trading a successful career for a quiet life of shuffleboard by the beach."[1]

Ness continues regarding Boomers, "Once they do decide to retire, that may not be the end of working either. While their grandparents may have retired into a life of leisure, many of today's active adults continue to work full or part-time jobs after retiring from their primary career. Despite being retirees, they may take on consulting work, turn a hobby into a second career or start their own new businesses."

In her insightful book, *The Third Chapter, Passion, Risk and Adventure in the 25 Years after Fifty*, Harvard sociologist Sara Lawrence-Lightfoot states that Boomers "do not want to retreat from their engagement in, or contribution to, society, even though they are eager to develop new kinds of activity, new daily rhythms, new habits of conduct and new sources of motivation and reward."[2]

New Active Lifestyle Trends

American retirees will continue to relocate to resort communities like those in Florida, Arizona or California, but many Boomers will be just as likely to stay near family and friends. According to one Trilogy LifeScape Survey, the *driving distance of family and friends* is considered to be the most important factor in choosing a retirement destination.[3]

Reversing the late 20th century migration from the cities to the new modern suburbs, Boomers are returning to urban living. Citing a 2010 AARP survey and analysis of the 2010 Census data by the real estate brokerage Redfin, Tara Bathrampour of the Washington Post suggests, "Many [Boomers] are empty nesters, and freed of the need to factor in school districts and yard sizes, they are gravitating to dense urban cores near restaurants, shops, movie theaters and Metro stations."[4]

Tired of mowing lawns, Boomers want to enjoy church, restaurants and entertainment venues within easy walking distance. A desire to be close to the vibrancy of city life has led many Boomers back to condos or row houses in the city.

In response, senior adult community developers have set their sights on innovative residential communities to appeal to active adults with diverse interests. For example, in my home city of Lancaster, PA, Landis Communities, an umbrella organization operating Landis Homes Retirement Community has created a thirty-six unit rental complex, Steeple View Lofts, designed for active adults aged fifty-five and older. This project brings city apartment rentals to those wanting to live in the bustling activity of a small city downtown rather than out in the quieter suburbs.[5]

A survey of more than 2,000 Boomers by Trilogy LifeScape revealed that Boomers are still "very active, adventurous and connected, ready to live life to the fullest," said Hal Looney, area president of Shea Homes Active Lifestyle Communities.[6] Regarding the future, 51% of those surveyed said that retirement is a time for re-invention and self-discovery. Only 8% see retirement as a time to play, while 59% revealed that they are looking forward to traveling. The survey also found that 43% percent look forward to pursuing new interests and hobbies, with 35% wanting lots of activities to choose from. Half of the survey participants cited an interest in having a more balanced lifestyle (51%) or becoming more active (46%).

Older Adult Boomer Myths

In 2008, when the first Boomers turned 62, the American Association for Retired Persons (AARP) Services and Focalyst identified common myths about the Boomer generation, noting that there are diverse segments within this gernerational group.[7]

The report addressed the following perceptions:

Myth–Boomers are retiring early.
   Reality–Only 11% plan to stop working entirely when they reach retirement age.

Myth–Boomers are downsizing their homes.
   Reality–Only 6% of Boomers are planning to be living in a smaller residence five years from now.

Myth–Most Boomers are married empty nesters.
   Reality–37% of Boomers still have children under 18 in the home, and a third are single.

Myth–Boomers are winding down with age.
   Reality–The typical Boomer regularly participates in an average of ten different activities.

Myth–Boomers are technologically challenged.

Reality–Boomers were in the workforce during the evolution of computers, e-mail and the Internet; 82% of Boomers use the internet and their online activities

Myth–Boomers are the "Me Generation".

Reality–70% say they have a responsibility to make the world a better place; Boomers are becoming the "we-generation" in later adulthood.

Ambition to Change the World

Each generation has its activists, whether for slavery's abolition, women's suffrage, or the end to an unpopular war. During the late 1960s young adult Boomers marched in the streets to express their outrage at the Vietnam conflict without today's Internet blogging and tweeting from the comfy sofa. Protest posters were hand-painted and carried, not posted on Facebook with the click of a mouse. Social media in the 1960s meant old-fashioned word-of-mouth, mimeograph flyers and the rotary telephone.

That is not to over glamorize the Boomer generation's ability to catalyze completely selfless social good. Within the bravado of anti-war activism was a hedonistic pursuit of pleasure, and Boomer's were sparking consumeristic economic changes. The Vietnam War ended and within a few years my 1970s college classmates were pursuing careers that would make the most money, not necessarily to make the world a better place. "What? You're majoring in psychology?" my peers questioned me. "You'll never get rich that way!"

Yet, whether for noble causes or self-serving ones, the Boomer

Whether for noble causes or self-serving ones, the Boomer generation was, and still is, characterized by a drive to change the status quo.

generation was, and still is, characterized by a drive to change the status quo. Change was no longer feared, it was expected. A Boomer chant of the idealistic 1960s declared, "Be realistic. Demand the impossible!"

Boomers Still Look for Causes

Aging boomers will continue to eagerly scan the landscape for challenges and opportunities to make a difference. According to the National Association of Boomers, "All [Boomers] are joined by an increased social awareness and a deep concern for not only their baby Boomer generation, but the nation and world as a whole."[8] Churches and non-profit ministries who want to engage Boomers will be wise to create new doorways of service opportunities.

Congregations that are active in community revitalization will be attractive, and for some Boomers volunteering to meet real human need through a local church will introduce them to the faith of that church. They may arrive to serve, and through this relationship they will discover the transformative whole-person work of Christ.

Barry, a pastor and leadership coach, speaks for many Boomers when he looks ahead, "I don't want to begin to coast to the finish line as I feel many begin to do. I don't want to stop learning, stop experiencing new things or be put on the shelf as irrelevant or unneeded. The most exciting to me will be to work but without as much pressure from the clock and my schedule but rather doing mostly what I feel I can do best and where I can offer the most. To me boredom is more frightening than anything. The world is too big and too exciting to drop out of life and just stay home more. I would like to spend more time traveling, learning and doing some of those things which I could not do because of my schedule in my work."

Astronaut John Glenn's return to space in the shuttle thirty-six years after his first historic flight seemed to inaugurate the Boomer view of aging. Fellow astronaut Gene Cernan noted that Glenn's trip had "probably done more for senior citizens than Viagra." Back on the ground Glenn proclaimed: "Just because you're up in years doesn't mean you don't have hopes and dreams and aspirations as younger people do."

Innovation Needed

In his book *Prime Time*, Marc Freedman states, "Next to travel, volunteering is the second highest priority for [the Boomer] generation." He sites a study by Peter Hart of the Experience Corps that found 40% of Boomer respondents were "very interested" or "fairly interested" in high commitment opportunities, such as half-time service projects. Freedman concludes that "most studies reveal that 'the new generation' of older Americans is planning to make volunteer work a central part of later life."

Most studies reveal that "the new generation" of older Americans is planning to make volunteer work a central part of later life.

He adds, "Given that the over-65 segment alone will swell to nearly 70 million over the next three decades, the potential size of this involvement is enormous."[9]

Freedman predicts that literally millions of new opportunities need to be developed to satisfy potential demand on the part of aging Boomers, and he urges that intensive innovation is needed. But, he laments, "Despite many new inventions — inventions that deserve to be taken on a much larger scale — I am convinced that we have yet to build the breakthrough institution." He continues, "Desperately needed is an entity that could speak to these individuals, the 95% who find nothing of interest at the local senior center, who aren't looking for bingo or adult day care, and who are unlikely to answer to the labels like 'the elderly.'"[10]

The Church's Opportunity

Brandon Hatmaker describes a troubling moment in his spiritual journey this way, "I hadn't really given up on faith in God, but I had almost given up faith in human ability to actually do something sincere, productive and unselfish when in an organized religious setting."[11] Now Hatmaker is a pastor shaping a local church to be missionally active and to be unselfishly productive.

Might Freedman's hoped for "breakthrough institution" be the Church? What if organized communities of faith across the nation took Freedman's challenge to mobilize Boomers' passion and skills? And what if Boomers all across local congregations organized to be a blessing and to help others find wholeness of life in Christ?

More Than a New "Seniors" Program

Generational-based ministry gained dramatic momentum because of the Boomers. The enormous crowd of Boomer teens led many churches in the 70s and 80s to create the modern "youth pastor" staff role. With so many teens milling around, churches seized the opportunity to engage them. As this large demographic bulge continued to age, new ministries emerged for "twenty-somethings," and subsequently young parent groups were created for the "thirty-somethings."

But it would be a mistake to respond with a "one-size-fits-all" senior program for Boomers within the local church. A classroom full of toddlers will play and interact with others in similar ways because they are all learning the same basic skills. In contrast, gather a roomful of older Boomers and some will have traveled to every continent while others never ventured far from their hometown. Some will have postgraduate degrees and others will hold expert craftsmanship awards.

Many Boomers are not interested in an exclusive "retirees" ministry. Most want to interact within inter-generational environments. A grandmother may have a passion to mentor young first-time mothers, or a retired businessman may want to encourage middle-aged entrepreneurs. In the past leaders of senior ministries may have functioned as travel agents for garden shows, but new leaders among older adult Boomers will more likely be *personnel directors* for service.

Speaking to the mayors of 42 cities around the world Ambassador James Joseph, stated, "[Policy-makers] should be asking not simply what social service should we provide, but how can we encourage and empower older adults to continue serving..."[12]

Thus, the focus of this book is not on developing a new, hipster "Boomer senior program," but rather to mobilize the wide diversity of Boomer experiences and skills in order to impact many areas of mission in the church and the community. The point is that Boomers won't be looking for a ministry focused on them, instead they will want to be *involved in* ministry, from worship service child care to free legal consultations to arranging homelessness relief and mentoring youth in practical life skills.

> *Boomers won't be looking for a ministry focused on them, instead they will want to be involved in ministry.*

In her book, *Baby Boomers and Beyond,* gerontology professor and active church volunteer Amy Hanson describes a VolunteerMatch study that showed more than half of adults over 55 are interested in volunteering. Hanson says, "The challenge is that many of them are having difficulty finding the right opportunity in which to share their skills and experience." She adds, "Aging Boomers will be looking for ways to use their personal and professional skills. Many of them will want to do more than fold bulletins or staple newsletters."[13]

Many Boomers do not intend to spend their retirement years walking the beach with a metal detector, but rather they expect to use their freedom to serve some grand purpose. And so local churches have the historic opportunity to engage thousands in the redemptive purposes of God. For followers of Jesus, a commitment to faith is a matter of life-long discipleship, including the post-career years. For the newcomer to faith, participating with the world-changing purposes of God is a profound new life-changing discovery. New followers of Jesus can anticipate an amazingly satisfying and fulfilling new experience in their post-career years.

Traditional doctrines on aging held that one's meaningful employment was simply sandwiched between the playfulness of childhood and the recreation of retirement. This Play/Work/ Play formula stated: "I worked hard all my life and now I get to go have fun, I earned it." Yet Boomers express doubt that teeing off on the golf course every day will bring the satisfaction and meaning they long for. So imagine a new doctrine that declares, "I worked hard and now I can encounter new satisfaction by using my life experiences to freely serve others."

Beyond Shuffeboard Boredom–A Boomer Vision

In his book *Generous Justice*, Tim Keller describes two basic kinds of service to others.[14]

> *Healing communities* – where people find refuge, safety, love and fellowship *within* the church community. This is *attractional* presence, people run to it, like a traveler to the glowing light of a warm house in a raging snowstorm.

> *Healers of communities* – where people find the church community coming among them. This is *incarnational*

presence, the church running to the neighborhood, like a parent to a crying child that has fallen off his bike.

If you are a Boomer, imagine helping to make your church a vibrant *healing community*, an attractive place for people to find love and wholeness.

Imagine helping to be a *healer of communities,* your towns and city impacted because you serve for something more than a salary, more than climbing the ladder in a career.

Imagine investing your new post-career flexibility of time and freedom to use your diverse talents to meet the needs of others as an act of grace.

> *Imagine investing your new post-career flexibility of time and freedom to use your diverse talents to meet the needs of others as an act of grace.*

Imagine a new phase of accomplishment without financial gain as a primary motivation.

Just ahead in Part II, we'll explore eight areas to help you shape your future as you ease toward a new season of meaningful retirement ministry engagement.

Your calling – What is my unique life purpose?
Your skills – What can I do?
Your stuff – What do I own?
Your insight – What do I know?
Your leading –When do I take initiative?
Your creativity – What can I make?
Your schedule – How much time do I have?
Your health – What physical abilities do I have?

This is the "workbook" section. You'll need a pencil to write down your self-assessment and discoveries, or journal your responses on your favorite eletronic device.

POST-CAREER DESIGN QUESTIONS

For the Pastor

Among your congregation participants, list the occupations and professions in which Boomers currently serve or have recently retired from.

How many have been leaders or managers in their field?

For the Boomer

Write a paragraph describing your overall, general anticipation of retirement, then share this with others. Completing these sentences may help.

- When I think about retirement I feel…

- My biggest fear about retiring is…

- The thing I look forward to the most is…

- My retirement will be different from my parents' experience in that I will…

- When considering volunteer work during retirement, I will look to _____ for meaningful placement. (The church? Non-profit charities? The government?)

PART II – Your Personal Assets

The righteous will flourish like palm trees;
they will grow like the cedars of Lebanon.
They are like trees planted in the house of the Lord,
that flourish in the Temple of our God,
that still bear fruit in old age
and are always green and strong.

Psalm 92:12-14 (GNB)

The chapters in Part II are designed to help you reflect more specifically on how God might bring your life-time of experiences together for an amazing new season of contribution to God's purposes.

Grab a pencil to jot down your responses. Open a journal notebook or power up your tablet or laptop so you can capture your ideas.

Respond to each chapter with prayer, inviting the Holy Spirit to guide you. Proverbs 16:9 reminds us, "You may make your plans, but God directs your actions. " (GNB)

Share you responses with others: your spouse, your pastor, and other family members. If you are part of a small group listen to each other and encourage one another along the journey to find meaningful engagement in your post-career season of life. Have fun unpacking the wonderful assets of your life.

CHAPTER THREE

My Calling – What is My Unique Life Purpose?

*A*t the basic level, every follower of Christ should be able to say, "I want to faithfully worship and serve God, encourage others in his church, and share the Good News of Jesus." This is the essential purpose shared around the world by every believer, from Hong Kong to London to Atlanta.

Yet each follower of Christ is also a specially designed member of the Body of Christ, crafted and called by God to a unique purpose to serve God's purposes in the world. This is your *personal life purpose*, God's assignment to you.

You likely have been pursuing a personal life purpose without knowing it. Just because you never wrote down a personal mission statement does not mean that you have no purpose in life. "Discovery" of your life purpose means you are looking for something that is probably already there, it may simply be hidden from your view.

So, first, a few affirmations about your unique calling.

Your Occupation is Not Your Identity

If you surrendered your life to Christ, you are a new creation in Christ. You are a child of God. Whether you are employed or not, whether you have a title or not, whether you receive a paycheck or not does not change your identity. You are a member of God's royal household, serving God's purposes. That is your identity. Every occupation, title, status, salary level, and public recognition is secondary, temporary and limited to this human lifetime. Only your identity in Christ is eternal.

Identifying Purpose is Not a One-day Process

Finding your personal life mission is not an intellectual problem to be solved in one day or even one week. It takes time to fully grasp what God's plan is for your specific residence on the earth. God takes you through years of experiences, then it all begins to add up. For many, by the time you reach your fifties, you can see a pattern in your life that is as unmistakable as the sunrise and sunset.

Your Uniqueness is God's Design

God uniquely fashioned you with a creative, sovereign design so that you could carry out his purposes.

God made no mistakes when he thought of you and he built in your preferences for what you find appealing, the skills that you can do easily, and the ideas that you understand immediately. God gave you physical and mental gifts through your parent's genetic code. God also gave you spiritual gifts through his Spirit when you surrendered your life to him. And God uniquely fashioned you with a creative, sovereign design so that you could carry out his purposes.

Every God-given Life Purpose is Significant

In enthusiasm for the things he or she appreciates a person might be tempted to think that his or her unique personal life purpose defines the most important thing any human could experience – *everyone should be like me*. On the other hand, a person might think his or her life purpose is unworthy because it lacks glamour or public recognition – *nobody should be like me*.

The fact is, every part of the Body of Christ is significant. Every mission given by God is a worthy assignment. Yours and mine might be different, but we are both crucial to God's plan.

Identifying Purpose Involves Complete Surrender to God

God is sovereign, and we are his willing, available servants. As Christians we claim Jesus as our Lord, our King of kings, our absolute master to whom we gladly submit. Such a devoted servant can never refuse a fresh or a surprising call of God simply because it doesn't fit a static decades-old life mission statement.

Yet, while God can use us any way he chooses, Scripture reveals many examples of how God consistently assigned people to specific lifelong tasks to accomplish his purposes throughout history. Discovering your life purpose is not meant to restrict you, but to release you to embrace the patterns that emerge during your lifetime. It is confirmation of God's uniquely designed assignment that you humbly receive and obey.

Take a look at the following Biblical examples and compose a possible sentence for each person.

Deuteronomy 31:1-8 What does Moses describe as Joshua's personal life purpose? Joshua might say, "My life purpose is to..."

Esther 4:11-17 What does Mordecai surmise is Esther's personal life purpose? Esther might say, "My life purpose is to..."

Jeremiah 1:1-10 What does the Lord define as Jeremiah's personal life purpose? Jeremiah might say, "My life purpose is to...

Luke 19:1-10 What does Jesus define as his own personal life purpose? Jesus might say, "My life purpose is to ...

Matthew 3:3; John 3:27-30 What does John describe as his personal life purpose? John might say, "My life purpose is to ...

Acts 26:12-18 What does Jesus define as Paul's personal life purpose? Paul might say, "My life purpose is to ...

Galations 2:7-10 What is affirmed as Peter's life purpose? Peter might say, "My life purpose is to ...

So Who Am I?

Separate yourself from positions and titles. Who are you at the core beyond the name plate on the office door? You may have held the title and responsibility of "CEO". But who are you without that title? An entrepreneur? A people organizer? A visionary communicator? You may have been a "Senior Pastor." Are you an encourager? A teacher? An administrator? Or maybe you were a "Teacher" in an academic environment. Are you a researcher? A mentor? A coach? A writer? Or maybe an "Assembly Technician" in manufacturing. Are you a supervisor or manager? A trainer? A precision worker? Regardless of the title, status, or pay scale, what are/were you good at?

You may have faithfully carried out your daily duties throughout your working days, whether at home or beyond, only pausing occasionally to think about whether you really "loved" what you were doing. Frederich Beuchner once said, "Your vocation |calling| is that place where your deep gladness meets the world's hunger."[1] The following questions may help you put your finger on your life calling underneath the outward positions and titles you might have held.

POST-CAREER DESIGN QUESTIONS

Prayerfully, invite God to bring clarity to your thoughts as you respond to the following.

Question 1

What is it that when I do it, I sense **God's pleasure?**
- What activity gives me satisfaction that God is delighted, and that it furthers what is on God's heart?
- What activity consistently makes me feel alive and exuberant in my walk with Christ?

Question 2

What is my life's **"north star"** that guides me when it's dark?
- When I am up against a wall what values come to the surface that motivate me to press on?
- What are the things that I am determined to pursue regardless of any hardship?
- During a time I faced adversity, what core convictions rose up within me?

Question 3

What are dreams or goals I have worked tirelessly for **regardless of financial obstacles?**
- To what cause(s) do I sacrifice financially because I believe in it so strongly? Where do I spend my discretionary income?
- What projects/causes are easy for me to raise finances for because I am passionate about their worthiness?

Question 4

For what is it that people most often seek help from **me especially?**
- Why do they seek me and not just anyone else; what is unique about what I have to offer? Is there a fruitfulness that accompanies me in that area?

Question 5

What **people** do I most feel called to serve?
- Among people that you served in the past years, identify ten people for whom you *really enjoyed* serving, it brought you great satisfaction!

1. _____
2. _____
3. _____
4. _____
5. _____
6. _____
7. _____
8. _____
9. _____
10. _____ .

- What patterns do I identify from the above list? What common, similar theme(s) describe these people? They are often people who need _____, something I can provide.

Question 6

If I were asked to deliver a speech to a national audience on any subject (and I had the courage to do so), what topic would I choose?

Question 7

Finish these sentences: **By the time I die**....

- I want to be known for

- I want to have helped

- I want to have completed

Question 8

What specific **Scripture verse(s)** move me emotionally every time I read it/them?
- What Scripture verse stirs me to action regardless if others are impacted?
- What Scripture verse or quote have I treasured over the years?

Question 9

In my present job/occupation what have I learned during the past year or two?

- In the area of human relations?

- What practical trade skills?

- What leadership or management skills?

- Have I discovered something new I enjoy doing?

- What insight have I gained through adversity?

Question 10

What have personality and occupational assessment inventories revealed about **unique patterns** in my life?

Strength finders _____
DISC profile _____
(http://personality-testing.info/tests/DISC.php)
Spiritual gifts _____
Myers/Briggs _____
Work preference inventory _____
(http://www.careerperfect.com/content/
career-planning-work-preference-inventory)
Other: _____
Other: _____

Question 11

What specific **"prophetic"** (predictive, hopeful, inspired) **words** have been spoken to me about my unique calling or purpose?

Question 12

Which **FIVE** of these 150 verbs are the most exciting and purposeful to me? Circle FIVE, do you see any patterns to your choices?

relax	complete	educate	gather	model	reclaim
speak	mold	acquire	compliment	embrace	generate
reduce	motivate	refine	demonstrate	compose	encourage
give	admonish	conceive	distribute	grant	provide
reflect	support	study	advance	confirm	engage
heal	negotiate	reform	preserve	sustain	affirm
connect	engineer	praise	alleviate	consider	enhance
host	debate	teach	regard	amplify	construct
serve	identify	organize	accomplish	team	nurture
dream	contact	enlighten	illuminate	participate	fight
comfort	help	ascend	continue	enlist	implement
launch	touch	tell	mediate	counsel	enliven
improve	perform	compel	translate	release	believe
create	entertain	improvise	bless	enthuse	inspire
travel	pray	resonate	understand	renew	brighten
defend	envision	instruct	process	respect	uphold
persuade	build	evaluate	integrate	decide	share
adopt	excite	intercede	prepare	resfresh	utilize
urge	cause	design	explore	involve	write
revise	validate	restore	choose	devise	express
labor	sacrifice	venture	investigate	collect	direct
extend	produce	safeguard	verbalize	visit	collaborate
discover	facilitate	lead	combine	discuss	finance
learn	manage	save	volunteer	satisfy	command
enable	forgive	listen	promote	search	work

My Sense of Life Purpose

It seems to me on (date) _____,
that God wants to use me to... (Q. 12 verb/action words)

_____

among... (including people I sense a call to serve from Q. 5)

_____

so that.... (what I hope to accomplish/achieve)

_____

_____

A Scripture verse that expresses my life purpose (from Q. 8) is...

Further Testing

Names of three people with whom I will share what I've identified for their feedback and confirmation:

- _____ (Date shared) _____
- _____ (Date shared) _____
- _____ (Date shared) _____

Purpose Pursuit

In what ways am I *now pursuing* this purpose? (apprenticeship, a mentor, employment, travel, training, formal education, etc.)

Additional ways I sense *God may want me to pursue* this purpose: (apprenticeship, a mentor, employment, travel, training, formal education, etc.)

CHAPTER FOUR

My Skills – What Can I Do?

*Y*ou need not be a rocket scientist to have meaningful skills; each skill in important. You may have specific vocational training or simply years of experience in a specific task. You may have specialized training or maybe you just learned something on your own by practice. Some of you may have certifications, licenses, or other authorization to practice in your career.

Diversity of Skills

Boomers have experienced a rich variety of work assignments, and the accompanying skills and cross industry knowledge

Many Boomers have experienced a lifetime of multiple jobs and occupations that have taught them a wide array of skills. According to a Department of Labor Report, the average Baby Boomer has held eleven jobs by age 44.[1] This mobility and transition is a marked change from previous generations that held the same position for thirty-five years in the same factory. It means that Boomers have experienced a rich variety of work assignments, and the accompanying skills and cross industry knowledge.

Jim, a retired entrepreneur who transitioned from camera repair to home construction to co-founding a heating and cooling business with his brother, Ken, offered his skills to his local church during its major building project. He volunteered for months as project coordinator and used his considerable business and mechanical skills to help renovate an old building into a beautiful and functional new worship facility.

Dorthea Glass, M.D., provides free care to working poor patients in a clinic in Stuart, FL, a small town north of Palm Beach. Retired from practice in physical medicine and rehabilitation, Dorthea serves with Volunteers in Medicine[2] and provides gross neurological evaluations and a listening ear as people describe their daily journey with pain. Protected by Florida state legislation that licenses retired volunteer doctors, Dorthea can serve people without malpractice litigation worry.

She says, "We have the luxury of practicing medicine the way we think it should be practiced—and without having to worry about the money side." She continues, "When I was working for the money I was so over-committed. I don't think I could do as good a job then as I can do now."[3]

In their book, *How to Finish the Christian Life*, father and son George and Donald Sweeting tell of an attorney, Doyle, who, upon retiring, came to his pastor and said, "Pastor, I want to serve as an unpaid member of the church staff and help with visitation."[4] The Sweetings call such people "retirement rebels," like Chris and Jane, who left a medical practice in Detroit and sold or gave away their furniture so they could invest their remaining years as medical doctors in Uganda bringing health care to remote villages.

During a vacation one summer we met a retired couple who travel in their RV across the nation looking for small rural churches where they stop, find the pastor, and ask if there is any practical way to help them. Do they need a roof fixed? A room painted? He said, "You know, little churches need encouragement. And what is life worth if not to help people?"

Sometimes new volunteer roles are completely unrelated to any job you've ever held. Tina, a retired nurse, became an instructor in an ESL (English as a Second Language) class that her church offers to the community. This can be a refreshing adventure to learn a totally new skill.

Looking Back to Give Forward

At other times, skills lie dormant from a much earlier part of life. For example, Sara Lawrence-Lightfoot describes a neighbor, Charles, who worked for years as a successful attorney with a prestigious law firm. When the firm was forced to merge with another firm, Charles called it quits. As he packed up his office he carefully wrapped a beloved photograph that he looked at longingly for years—a picture of him at age eight standing with dirt smudged face with his mother in their North Carolina garden.

Now retired, Charles traded his sleek business suit for jeans and a sweatshirt and began to shape a garden in front of his city brownstone. Within months, Charles was volunteering at a neighborhood park, then a children's art center planting trees and shrubs. Now he assists in a large city garden where Chinese residents grow vegetables. By looking back, Charles found a way to give forward. Charles went back to something old and embarked in a fresh new adventure at the same time. Lawrence-Lightfoot calls this "Looking back to give forward."[5]

Duplicate Your Skills in Someone Else

Often we simply need to be good stewards of what we already have in our skill bank. Jesus told the story of a man who went on an extended trip and put three men in charge of all he owned. (Matthew 25:14-30)

The man knew what each of his managers could do and he delegated responsibility according to their ability. He handed five thousand coins to the first servant, two thousand to the second, and one thousand to the third. Then he left town.

The manager with five thousand coins used them to earn five thousand more. The one with two thousand coins did the same and earned two thousand more. But the guy with one thousand coins dug a hole and simply hid his master's money in the ground. When the master returned, he was delighted with the first two managers who had doubled what was entrusted to them, and he promptly promoted them.

The guy who had simply buried his share did not fare as well. His pitiful excuses fell flat and only added to his master's outrage. The wasteful manger was booted out as a lazy good-for-nothing.

The point Jesus seems to be making was not the actual dollar accomplishments, otherwise the first manager would have won the day. Jesus is telling us about God's delight

God is thrilled when you duplicate your gift.

in any person who simply doubles that which God has given him or her. God is thrilled when you duplicate your gift.

So, if you play a musical instrument, teach someone else. One guitar player is now two guitar players. You have doubled the number of guitarists on the face of the earth. If you can sew clothes, train someone else on the sewing machine. If you can invest or garden or build furniture, teach someone else that skill. And while you're at it, why not train four or five people?

What basic life skill might you duplicate in someone else's life? How might you mentor a person in skills that could lift them from poverty? One woman taught young girls how to shop at discount stores, helping them learn to stretch their dollars through buying dent and bent items, generic brands and slightly outdated, but still very safe, groceries. Another man noticed a boy throwing away bank checks because he had no bank account. He helped the youth open a checking account so he could cash checks when he was paid.

One Christmas my wife, Carol, taught a young single mother how to roast a turkey. On Christmas Day, we left our house so the young woman could invite her extended family to our home for a holiday meal she had prepared on her own. The meal was a success and she remembers this accomplishment with pride.

The eBay Factor

Many people will have multiple skills to offer, but then there is the rotary phone installer who realizes his skills are simply no longer needed. OgilvyOne Chairman and CEO, Brian Fetherstonhaugh, put it this way, "Think of your eBay factor. Say to yourself: 'If at age 60, I was put up for auction on eBay, who would bid for me?' If neither a paying organization nor a not-for-profit would, go do something about it to make yourself more valuable."[6] Fetherstonhaugh's challenge is that even if you have limited skills, you can do something about it. You might have to learn a new skill, and many Boomers are doing just that.

If you spent your entire career repairing 8-track tape decks and you think your skills are obsolete and useless, take heart! Take an inventory of your skills, then move on to the next chapters where we will discuss other assets you have beyond physical skills alone.

POST-CAREER DESIGN QUESTIONS

List your "primary" skills, those you have training, employment experience, certification, licensing, etc.:

List your "secondary" skills, such as hobbies, recreational pursuits, or extra-career short term jobs or ones held earlier in life:

List skills that you would like to enhance and receive more training or practice.

CHAPTER FIVE

My Stuff – What Do I Own?

According to a 2013 *BabyBoomer-Magazine* article, members of the Boomer generation:

- Have more discretionary income (wealth) than any other age group.
- Control 70% ($7 trillion) of the total net worth of American households.
- Own 80% of all money in savings and loan associations.
- Spend more money disproportionately to their numbers.
- Are not fanatically loyal to brands.
- Account for a dramatic 40% of total consumer demand.[1]

Boomers are a huge target for marketing, and all that discretionary income is in the cross hairs of the advertising industry. In 2012, Americans spent $206 billion on consumer electronics, with the average household spending $1,312 per year. But according to the EPA, we discard 1.05 million mobile devices every day, at a rate of 731 units per second! In 2011, we generated 3.4 million tons of e-waste in the U.S.[2]

With the turnover of new media and computer devices, consumers are left with a nagging buyer's anxiety, should I buy now or wait for the new version? If I do buy now, I'll regret it in six months. But waiting only delays the same dilemma all over again. *Planned obsolescence* is now an industry standard practice, where a product is designed for a short life, after which it will be unfashionable or will no longer function.

By now many in the Boomer generation have figured out that they can not buy happiness by accumulating more stuff. On the contrary, you do not have to be rich to have plenty. You do not have to be materially affluent to have abundance. And you need not have an oversized garage to have a full life.

According to Bill Ness, of 55places.com, Boomers are reaching the age when they are inclined to spend less on accumulating more "stuff."[3] Ness also observes that, having filled their homes and raised their children, Boomers often turn more toward buying *experiences* than physical items. Spending turns toward travel, eating out, sports, concerts or lifelong learning classes. During conversations at the small city café that Carol and I helped to start, philosophical Boomer customers would remind us, "I'm not just here to buy a product, but an experience."

> *By now many in the Boomer generation have figured out that they can not buy happiness by accumulating more stuff.*

Financial Anxiety

The American Dream fantasy of long leisurely days on the golf course can easily be shaken by volatility in the stock market and evaporating pension plans. Financial anxiety is high among many Boomers as they look ahead, and accordingly a stack of books have been written on financial management and security. Some are alarmist, like James Bacon, Jr.'s *Boomergeddon: How Runaway Deficits and the Age Wave Will Bankrupt the Federal Government and Devastate Retirement for Baby Boomers Unless We Act Now*. Other books are more practical.

To stay focused on the broader purposes of this book we'll leave financial planning specifics to these other experts. An Internet search, or better, an appointment with a trusted financial advisor will yield ample resources to plan your financial portfolio. The reality is, the Boomer who has assumed money will buy a satisfying retirement may be forced to reconsider a better mooring.

Some retirees who have spent years planning for their financial provision may have counted too much on money to give retirement its meaning. After a few weeks of enjoying financial freedom and spending money on recreation and eating at restaurants, such retirees can feel disappointed and lost.

On the other hand, people with small financial nest eggs might assume that they have very few options, only to discover activities of great significance that do not require money. Financial anxiety is rooted in the perceived gap between what I expect to purchase and the money I have to spend. Rethinking my retirement spending requirement can not only lead to more peace, but more vision for how to help others rather than to focus primarily on myself.

Older Boomers and Giving

There is a popular perception that the Boomer generation is self-centered with their money. But in his book, *One Church, Four Generations*, Gary McIntosh states, "On the contrary, Boomers are less ego-centric as one might assume. Like all generations, as the Boomers have aged, they have substantially increased their giving to charitable organizations." He adds, "Since they are concerned for causes and are highly relational, they want to give money to organizations that prove they are doing something of great value for people. It also means Boomers are more likely to give financially to a ministry that effectively communicates a clear mission and strong vision (a big cause)."[4]

A 2013 Blackbaud study of several generations found that Boomers give 43% of all charitable dollars donated.[5] This is not surprising since the Boomers are such a large percentage of the population. However, the study found that 72% of Boomers gave to charity in 2012, substantially higher than the 59% from GenXers, those born after 1964. The study quotes Pam Loeb, a principle of Edge Research, "The majority of nonprofit marketing spend and tactics are focused on mature donors." He adds, "However, we are starting to see a shift as Boomers become the dominant force in charitable giving and will remain so for quite some time."[6]

If you are a Boomer, do these reports about increased giving reflect your use of money? Are you increasing charitable giving as you grow older? Are you prepared to find meaning in more than the accumulation of money and "stuff?"

First-hand Involvement

A wealthy man once came to Jesus. "Teacher," he asked, "what good thing must I do to receive eternal life?"

Jesus responded, "Go sell all and give to the poor, then follow me." (Matthew 19:21; Luke 18:22) Jesus did not say, "Give money to my non-profit food bank so I can feed the poor." Instead he essentially instructed, "Get involved first-hand!" It seems Jesus wanted this well-resourced man to get exposed to poverty, to experience human need, and in so doing he might comprehend what inheriting "lasting life" was all about.

Jesus never implied to the man, "Go repent of your sin of wealth and stop making money." Rather, to paraphrase, I believe Jesus was saying, "What amazing resource do you have? The one thing you've yet to experience is the exhilaration of bringing life and justice to the disadvantaged. When you give a child a meal and see the joy on her face, then you'll *want* to follow me into the world!"

Selling possessions was expected of *all* disciples, and Jesus was not just being cynical with one rich man. Jesus taught, "Life is more than food or clothing." (Luke 12:33) Rather Jesus was saying to the man of means, "That's what my followers do, they get profoundly involved with the poor! Are you ready for that?"

Inter-generational Mission Trips

If Boomers are weary of buying "stuff" and want more experiences, the church can be poised to catalyze experiences among the least, the lost, and the last that can be life changing. To the aging Boomers with all that discretionary income, Jesus may be saying "Go spend time among the poor and put your stuff to work," Jesus says."

Boomers generally would like Jesus' challenge to get involved first-hand. They like to give finances to causes where they will have a personal connection.

In many churches, mission trips are a regular summer youth activity, but increasingly churches are noticing the Boomer generation's interest in these trips. Short term service trips, both domestic and international, provide a great opportunity for multiple generations to serve together for a worthy cause. Our daughter, Audra and her husband, Jared have led several international teams that included Boomer parents and their children.

Re-purposing our Stuff

Some of our material assets simply need to be put to work in a new purpose

Some of our material assets simply need to be put to work in a new purpose. For example, many Boomers are still caring for their aging parents while considering their own retirement. Lloyd, at age 56, with his wife, Elaine, renovated their home to include in-law quarters for their parents. But with the future in mind, Lloyd's children advised him to design a living space that he would eventually use.

My wife, Carol, and I use extra bedrooms in a private lower level of our home for guests. Others use extra rooms for college student lodging, or they offer a room for people who want a quiet retreat day.

Our homes are not the only asset that can be re-purposed. Tools that we once relied on for employment now may hang idle in the garage. Can these be used for new volunteer projects? If not, why not pass these tools on to someone younger who could use them for a livelihood to feed their family?

There are three basic ways to re-purpose and de-clutter from material possessions:

Throw it out/recycle it – Some of our accumulation no longer serves its original purpose, but could be remade into something useful. Our daughter Audra recycles clothes into chic infinity scarves and gives the sales proceeds to support the fight against human sex trafficking. (See https://www.facebook.com/BindingLoveScarves)

Other stuff simply takes up space, and space is an asset that could be re-purposed. Imagine an uncluttered attic that could be used as temporary storage for a family away on a two-year mission assignment who cannot afford to pay for a commercial storage unit.

Share it – Loan an item to someone who has a temporary need for a short-term project but cannot afford to purchase the item that you have. For example, you might have the power tools a friend or neighbor could use to renovate their bathroom. Ken and Joann share their RV with church leaders to enable a restful vacation.

Donate it – Take sharing to another step by giving away complete ownership of something that would be better used by someone else. Look around your community for a Goodwill or Salvation Army thrift shop or a Habitat for Humanity Re-Store. Many non-profit ministries and churches accept your donations to both provide low cost items to the public as well as revenue for their ministries.

Sell it – In many communities garage sales and Craig's List are very effective ways to turn unused accumulations into cash, funds that can be invested in *experiences*, not just more *stuff*.

Take Inventory

Jesus instructed his followers, "Watch out and guard yourselves from every kind of greed; because your true life is not made up of the things you own, no matter how rich you may be." (Luke 12:15 GNB)

In addition to money, as powerful a tool as it is, we Boomers have many other things that we've accumulated. Don uses his RV to travel to help poor rural churches. His intention is to sell his Texas home so he and his wife can do this full time.

Take an inventory of what you actually have. Start in your garage, or kitchen or basement! What is collecting dust from unuse? What valuable assets do you have that can be useful to others?

- A home, maybe spare bedrooms
- Lawn and gardening equipment
- Construction tools
- Vehicles, cars, trucks, trailers
- Craft, woodworking, sewing tools
- Auto repair tools,
- Tools from your working trade
- Kitchen equipment
- Clothes, sports gear.

What stuff have I accumulated? What can I donate? Re-purpose? Or sell, because I no longer need it, and so reallocate the money to a new use?

POST-CAREER DESIGN QUESTIONS

List things you own that you could *share*, make available for others to use:

List things you own that you could *donate* to someone or an organization that could make better use of it:

List things you own that you could *sell*, so that funds can be re-allocated to meet a need: (To what projects would your proceeds go?)

CHAPTER SIX

My Insight – What Do I know?

Intellectual Capital

*M*ore valuable than money is your *intellectual capital*. History, language, travel experiences, reading, knowledge of other cultures – all these are mental deposits that have been accumulating for decades. The study cited in Chapter Four that indicated that the average Baby Boomer has held eleven jobs by age forty-four means that many Boomers will have knowledge in multiple fields.

Gary, a retired strategic planning consultant, volunteered to walk alongside a college campus church reorganize and re-vision into new strategies for effectiveness. His knowledge of how organizations work brought significant wisdom into planning meetings with this church team.

Bruce, a pastor, expressed his hope for interaction with a younger generation of leaders, "Ideally, they would seek me to be a mentor and to assist them in any way I could to carry out the work of ministry. Practically, we often look at the older men as out of touch with current realities, or having a vision from the past rather than one that looks to the future. So I wouldn't be surprised if I were simply left alone." Many leaders echo Bruce's desire to effectively mentor others with the insight gained in life, especially passing to a younger generation useful understanding learned over years of mistakes and successes.

Why would others seek our counsel? Why would someone want to be mentored? Some have suggested that people look for advice for one of three reasons:

- They are curious – What you know seems intriguing.
- They are discouraged – What they know isn't working (and what you know seems to be working.)
- They are trusting – You are a friend, so anything you say is valuable.

Live Faith Out @ Work, Inc. lists ten reasons why people would search for coaching in their work or for their personal lives:

1. Something is at stake (a challenge, stretch goal or opportunity), and it is urgent, compelling or exciting.
2. There is a gap in knowledge, skills, confidence, or resources.
3. A big stretch is being asked or required, and it is time sensitive.
4. There is a desire to accelerate results.
5. A course correction is needed in work or life due to a setback.
6. An individual has a style of relating that is ineffective or does not support achievement of one's personally relevant goals.
7. There is lack of clarity, and there are choices to be made.
8. The individual is extremely successful, but success has brought new problems.
9. Work and life are in conflict resulting in unwanted consequences.
10. One has not identified his or her core strengths and how best to leverage them.

11. There is a desire for work and life to be less complicated. There is a need and a desire to be better organized and more self-managing.[1]

If one or more of these needs are present, there will likely be a high interest in seeking out an older person for help.

Passing on Knowledge

Dale Stoll, a church planter, life coach and friend, describes two ways to pass on knowledge, through a combination of both *mentoring* and *coaching*.

Mentoring – Taking knowledge that I have gained through a life-time of experiences and passing that information on to you; offering to share with you *what God has deposited into me*.

Coaching – Drawing out of you the knowledge and skills you may already have in you; offering to help you discover *what God has deposited into you*.

Of course, the catch is in knowing how to effectively apply these two. Discernment is needed for when one should mentor (tell you *my* solutions) and when one should coach (ask you about *your* solutions).

Sometimes the knowledge gained by your experiences provides clues that can help a younger person avoid a damaging and painful pitfall. Some knowledge is universal in its application; it is timeless wisdom that is passed as a gift from one generation to another.

However, at other times, your experiences may be obsolete because of a different time and context, or you have different gifts and personality, and you will help the person more by taking on a listening posture. Your past experiences and insights might interfere with new realities. Or your approach from your giftedness might actually be less effective than a new approach from differing gifts and personality. So instead of telling a person what to do, you ask, "When you prayed what did God seem to be saying to you about a course of action?" Rather than injecting your opinion, you ask the person, "Based on what you understand about this situation, what do you think is the best course of action?"

Larry Kreider's book, *The Cry for Spiritual Mothers and Fathers: The Next Generation Needs You to be a Spiritual Mentor* (Regal), provides a wealth of practical wisdom on developing trusted influential relationships.

The Power of Story

Jesus passed on knowledge through stories. Many of the people we consider great communicators are master sto-ry-tellers. If you are exploring how to find significance in retirement read stories, watch videos, interview new retirees.

To inspire and mobilize Boomers, congregations can create blogs that tell stories of retiree's activities and the significance of their endeavors. Stories about both part-time and vol-

Many of the people we consider great communicators are master story-tellers.

unteer work must be told to reinforce the reality that a job's value is not merely determined by its salary. Volunteers may be given business cards, provided with office space, and/or given decision-making roles at staff meetings. They may simply work solo out of their home. Regardless of the perks or setting, it is the story of what they accomplish that matters, not how much they were paid or whether they had office space.

An outreach focused church will promote stories of service within the broader community, not just about internal church maintenance activities. How many volunteer hours do retirees from your congregation log in the community? The more hours, the more stories to tell! Are your retirees involved in both faith-based and in secular organizations? Outreach oriented churches love stories of how volunteers demonstrate Christ's love among those who don't yet know the grace of Christ.

We need role models for every stage of life, and stories tell us about them. A child looks up to the sixth grader, and the high schooler admires those cool college students. The middle-aged look up to successful senior leaders in their field. Likewise, retirees need role models who provide an admired example of significant engagement in service; they need to hear stories of those walking just ahead in life's journey.

Write a Book

Retirement might be a time to write a book to pass on your knowledge. You may have expressed many opinions about all kinds of topics throughout your working life, but there is something about aging that tempers one's dogmas. Things start to simplify. I've heard older, scholarly theologians say quietly "Just give me Jesus." Now that you are older and wiser, what simple truths have emerged for you?

Lisa anticipates her post-CEO days, "I'd also enjoy having additional time to write about the many things God has taught me through life and through ministry." Keith, a long-time leadership consultant, related to me his desire to write during retirement, "Writing is one way to leave a legacy of truth, and the slower pace of retirement lends itself to more discretionary time for writing legacy like materials."

What could you write; what genre would you choose? Might it be a training manual from a career skill you have? A curriculum workbook? A biography of someone with whom you worked that you admired? Or a novel that might create a story of human meaning and redemption? If you've written before, it might be time for a sequel, a second volume, or a revised version.

After writing several books I now understand what other authors have told me -- you can feel when a book "wants to be written." It can be a holy moment, when you sense God wants to say something through you, certainly not in place of the canon of inspired Scripture, but as an expression of his ongoing living Presence.

The publishing industry has changed dramatically in recent years. No longer do you need to be a famous professor, or have garage space to stack thousands of books you hope to sell to friends. Self-publishers can create high quality print on demand books. With more people using electronic book reading devices, Kindle's free publishing is readily available. (See https://kdp. amazon.com)

Relational Capital

Knowledge may also include "relational capital", that is, *who* do you know? What influence do you have with business leaders, elected officials, international leaders, or educators?

Sometimes the most valuable asset you can offer is to connect someone you know *that has a need* with someone else you know *that has a resource*. Helping someone expand their network of relationships is a gift. During the start-up of the city café, those of us who were older on our intergenerational team had great connections with people who had discretionary funds to invest.

You might know of someone who has the skill or experience needed for a project, or a medical professional or counselor who helped you, or an instructor who has researched a topic. You might be well known and respected in your community, and that trust equity allows you to advocate for someone with less experience.

From Ignorance to Action

Another body of knowledge is simply what we have witnessed in life. Some events don't stick in our memory while others remain vivid in our minds, calling us to do something. The progression toward any kind significant action begins with exposure to something new, and can be charted in six stages:

Stage zero – *ignorance*, I have no inkling of the facts.
Stage one – *exposure*, I become aware of something.
Stage two – *interest*, I want to know more about this.
Stage three – *concern*, this is something important.
Stage four – *burden*, something must be done!
Stage five – *engagement*, I'm going to get involved.
Stage six – *sacrifice*, I'm willing to suffer, even die, for this cause.

The personal writings of David Livingston reveal his anger at the horrors of the slave trade as it spread to the areas of Africa where he worked. His biographer vividly described Livingston's passion, that the thought "warmed his blood and he felt like a Highlander with his hand on the claymore." What Livingstone witnessed shaped his life work.

Livingstone did not stall at the exposure stage, or even at the concern stage. Cynics can easily rant, "Isn't it awful, something must be done!" but too often they expect someone else will do something. On the other hand, real world changers are willing to get involved to the point of great sacrifice. For Christians, the narrative of Christ's journey through the cross to redeem the world provides deep inspiration, the ultimate engagement in a world problem.

Christ's journey through the cross to redeem the world provides deep inspiration, the ultimate engagement in a world problem.

74

Or, you may have gained some insight into the nuances of the life-style of other people groups. You may have witnessed first hand the daily routines, the art, the food and music of other cultures. In their book, *Shaping a Life of Significance for Retirement,* Hansen and Hass tell the story of Mark, who lived in various parts of the world because of his work with a multi-national corporation. Now retired, Mark uses his considerable cross-cultural knowledge to lead his church's international mission efforts. He arranges trips by teams to conduct medical mission projects in foreign locations.[2]

You may have seen abuse first hand or the effects of poverty. As you witnessed the world around you, at some point you might have thought, "One day, *if I had time,* I would do something about that!" That discretionary time might be just ahead. What needs have you witnessed that leave you no longer innocent?

Adding to Your Knowledge

Proverbs 1:5 says, "...let the wise listen and add to their learning, and let the discerning get guidance." Few processes in life have a more profound impact than our capacity to learn. Maturity in every area comes through learning, from learning to tie shoes, ride a bike, cook a meal, fix a car, solve a physics equation, or perform surgery. Learning is a lifelong endeavor. A college in my home region advertises, "What did you learn today?"

Few processes in life have a more profound impact than our capacity to learn.

Instead of shying away from technology, retirees today often embrace emerging trends. This is especially true of Boomers who were among the first to grow up with TV and discovered the wonders of personal computers. A typical retiree's home may include some state-of-the-art technology including home theater systems and wireless networking. They keep in touch with family and friends through social networking and have smart phones with the latest apps.

While local colleges and universities have programs geared to older students, retirees also have the flexibility of online learning programs. Boomers aren't afraid of using the Internet to expand their knowledge.

We learn by three basic ways: by watching (visual); by touching and doing (kinesthetic), and by listening and hearing (auditory). Most of us, 75 percent in fact, are visual learners, that is, we get it after we see it. "Do you see what I mean?" "Oh, I get the picture." "Can you draw me a map..."

Where will you learn best? Reading a book? Watching a video? Hearing a lecture? Getting hands-on experience? Simple on-line learning style assessment tools, (see *http://sunburst. usd.edu/~bwjames/tut/learning-style/stylest.html*) can reveal your preferred learning style and can help you engage in new educational activities.

Some things we can't learn: how to breathe under water, how to fly by flapping one's arms. And there are some things we could learn, we just refuse to: how to play chess, how to plant a garden, or how to skydive from 5,000 feet. The old saying, "You can't teach an old dog new tricks," is often an excuse for stubbornness, or at least a form of laziness. It is perilous to conclude that nothing new can be learned.

A few years ago an elderly neighbor, Don, was nearing death from cancer and we spent some time talking about faith. " I don't believe there is a God, or an afterlife," Don stated resolutely. "I believe we all just turn back into dust." I invited him to consider the alternative of the Living Creator God who loved him, knew him, and wanted a relationship with him. I urged Don to think about the Biblical revelation that gives an expectancy of meeting his Creator at death, and acknowledging how Jesus has redemptively made a way for us imperfect mortals to be with God in eternity.

Don smiled politely, but passively, and said, "Yeah, I've heard that story—never believed it—and I'm too old to change my mind now about things like that." A few days later Don was dead. I grieved at his refusal to learn when his eternity was at stake.

Life-long Learning

Cognitive exercises, that is, activities that require thinking, reasoning and remembering, have been shown to help brain health and functioning. A Scientific American article on brain exercises put it this way, "A book a day may keep dementia away."[3] As we Boomers grow older mental exercises will become as important as other physical workouts.

Some time ago an Aircraft Owners & Pilots Assoc. monthly magazine title caught my eye: "Good Pilots Are Always Learning." My family physician echoed this ambition, "a medical doctor must always be learning." It is reassuring, whether flying at 30,000 feet or on the operating table that professional pilots and surgeons are always learning. But how about the rest of us? Should we not always be learning in our journey through life? A college professor once told me that, as an educator, his success depended more on his capacity to learn than on his capacity to teach.

The Biblical word *disciple* could be simply defined as an "attentive learner" specifically from another person. Jesus chose twelve "learners." After the outpouring of the Holy Spirit at the Feast of Pentecost Scripture records that the number of "learners" increased. Followers of Jesus never stop being learners. Consider how the following verses would read if this alternative phrase is inserted:

"By this will all people know that you are my |attentive learners|, if you love one another." (John 13:35)

"This is to my Father's glory, that you bear much fruit, showing yourself to be my [attentive learners.]" (John 15:8)

"And the [attentive learners] were filled with joy and the Holy Spirit." (Acts 13:53)

Five Ways to L.E.A.R.N.

The following list is elementary, and if you are an older Boomer you've been pursuing these disciplines for many years. So consider these Scriptures as a quick review of five basic, but essential, skills for life-long learning.

Listen – Jesus said, "It is written in the Prophets: 'They will all be taught by God.' Everyone who *listens* to the Father *and learns* from him comes to me." (John 6:45, italics added) Listening is the most basic way to gain more information. Arguments can quickly turn into learning experiences with a simple "tell me more" response instead of launching into one's own opinion.
Want to learn something? Listen.

Expect – When Moses felt unprepared for a new task, God promised him, "Now go; I will help you speak and will teach you what to say." (Exodus 4:12) Moses had to get started with an expectation that he would learn more along the way. His posture had to be, "I'm going to learn something today.
Want to learn something? Be expectant.

Ask – One day Jesus was praying in a certain place, and when he finished, one of his disciples said to him, "Lord, teach us to pray, just as John taught his disciples." (Luke 11:1) They asked, and so Jesus did! In fact Jesus was so delighted that they had asked to be taught that a short time later he exclaimed, "So I say to you: *Ask* and it will be given to you; seek and you will find; knock and the door will be opened to you. For everyone who *asks receives*..." (Luke 11:9-10, italics added) Children are natural at asking, and they discover early in their development that they can learn volumes with simple questions. Why, Mom? Where, Dad? How, Grandpa?

Want to learn something? Ask around!

Reflect – Wise King Solomon pondered, "I applied my heart to what I observed and learned a lesson from what I saw." (Proverbs 24:32) We do not learn solely by the mere experience of an event, rather, we learn by pausing to *review that experience* and to consider its meaning and consequence. Reflective contemplation about an event is the workshop of new discovery, understanding and insight.

Want to learn something? Stop and reflect.

Nourish – Jesus once invited those who would follow him, "Take my yoke upon you and *learn from me*, for I am gentle and humble in heart, and you will find rest for your souls." (Matthew 11:29, italics added) Jesus promises that walking alongside Him will lead to soul-fulfilling learning. If you want to learn you will want a reliable "news feed," something other than bombastic radio talk shows, cynical pundants, and tabloid junk food stories about Elvis sightings on Mars. In contrast, wise choices in nonfiction and biographical reading, museums, galleries, historical documentaries, formal and informal class-rooms, and field trips all can enrich your knowledge.

Want to learn something? Nourish your mind.

Knowledge of the Good News

Many aging Boomers face retirement without a sense of grand purpose, without awareness of God's great mission on the earth. Without daily conversation with their Creator through prayer, they are left to navigate the aging experience on their own, scrounging for crumbs of guidance from afternoon TV psychologists.

If you are a devoted follower of Jesus, then your knowledge of the redeeming love of Jesus is the most important eternal truth you know. A 2001 study by George Barna revealed that people over the age of fifty are one of three groups *most receptive* to the Good News of Christ.[4] If this remains true today, then Boomers have an amazing opportunity, and a loving responsibility, to introduce their peers to Jesus.

If "Christendom" – a society dominated by the Christian worldview in its institutions and civil affairs – no longer defines America as we noted in Chapter One, then it is urgent that Boomers communicate a vibrant faith to the next generation who will live and work in a post-Christian American culture. Younger generations will need older adult collaboration on how the Christian story can be humbly re-introduced to future Americans who have no knowledge of the Christian worldview.

Stuart Murray observes regarding the distant future era of the Boomers' great-grandchildren, "Forty years on, both renewal and evangelization may be easier. As memories of Christendom fade, as the generation of church members dies for whom the final years of Christendom were disappointing, and as the snapshots with which this chapter opened become commonplace, resistance to change may be less, post-Christendom forms of church and mission may be emerging and there may be greater openness to a story that is quite unknown."[5]

One faith story you know more about than anyone else is your own personal spiritual journey. If you have experienced the redemption and transformation of Christ, then you have a first-hand account of the meaning of Christian faith. You are a witness to the reality of the Good News. To effectively tell this story, learn to tell your journey in chapters, that is, a segment or event in your life where you had a profound encounter with God. (See **Appendix A** for a faith story writing guide.) This may be your most profound knowledge asset!

POST-CAREER DESIGN QUESTIONS

List general topics that you know something about through experience, study, research, observation, etc.:

In what way might you offer to share this knowledge with others?

- If I would write a book it would be about...

- If I would teach a class it would be about...

- If I would tutor or mentor an apprentice I would most like to help them learn to...

CHAPTER SEVEN

My Initiative – When do I Lead?

*D*on't skip this chapter if you think that you are NOT a leader. Everyone leads something. You might lead a large group, a team, or just one other co-worker. You might be the first to start singing "happy birthday" at a party, or you might take your child by the hand to cross the street. You might be the first to introduce yourself to a newcomer.

The question is not, "do I lead?" but rather *"when* do I lead?" When do I take the initiative, when do I go first, when do I guide others? When do I show the way?

> *The question is not, "do I lead?" but rather "when do I lead?"*

The Early Church Experience

Paul's letter to the Ephesian church (4:11) lists five functions – apostles, prophets, evangelists, pastors and teachers – that describe ways leaders equipped the early Church to do its work. Identifying these "five-fold" functions has been helpful for people to understand their own unique contribution to the Christian movement.

Apostles helped communities of faith to mulitply.
Prophets helped the church know God's direction.
Evangelists spread the message of Christ.
Pastors and *teachers* helped people mature in Christ.

Some local churches have used these "five-fold" functions to organize their leadership teams. Yet while these are important tasks, you might not think any of these five fit your skills. If you are not a "prophet" or "pastor" does that mean there is no place to lead? How do these five function in business, or in community service?

Another description of the first generation church from the book of Acts suggests an alternative practical approach to finding your place of service and of leadership, not only in church settings but also in your community. Acts 2:41-47 records the Church's primary activities.

Those who accepted [Peter's] message were baptized, and about three thousand were added to their number that day. They devoted themselves to the apostles' teaching and to the fellowship, to the breaking of bread and to prayer.

Everyone was filled with awe, and many wonders and miraculous signs were done by the apostles. All the believers were together and had everything in common. Selling their possessions and goods, they gave to anyone as he had need.

Every day they continued to meet together in the temple courts. They broke bread in their homes and ate together with glad and sincere hearts, praising God and enjoying the favor of all the people. And the Lord added to their number daily those who were being saved.

From this account we can identify five simple, yet profoundly life-giving activities within the fledgling, Spirit-filled faith community.

Apostles' teaching – Learning from a trusted source.
Fellowship – Building meaningful relationships.
Breaking of bread – Tangibly honoring Jesus' death.
Prayer – Praising and petitioning God together.
Sharing of goods – Meeting the physical needs of others.

All five of these simple activities are essential for any person following Jesus. However, when faith communities participate in these activities together, servant-hearted people are needed to lead the rest of us into these Acts 2 life-giving experiences.

Five Life-Giving Functions (that need leaders)

These five functional "Acts 2" activities transcend age, culture, race, and social status. Why? Because they engage a universal set of human needs. Consider the following:

People hunger for insight–"…apostles' teaching…"

People will scratch around for ideas to help them make sense of everyday life. They'll watch Oprah, Dr. Phil, Dr. Oz., read newspapers, go to seminars, consult astrologers, and pay for psychotherapy. Are you a teacher, someone with wisdom from God that addresses this hunger for insight?

The old "chalk and talk" methods, where a professor filled the blackboard with massive amounts of content is being replaced by a need for *content in context* instruction, that is, an emphasis on how to apply information. Can you mentor someone from your experience? Could you tutor someone or apprentice him or her in a practical setting? How might you offer yourself as a volunteer to teach or train others?

People hunger for relationships–"…and to the fellowship…"

People long for meaningful relationships with people they

can trust, with people that will love them and help them find the best in life. Are you a relational person that enjoys meeting newcomers? Do you make friends easily? Do you pursue relationship building?

In the late 1990s Win Arn and his son, Charles, conducted a study of 42,000 people asking, "What or who was responsible for your coming to Christ and your church?" 75-90 percent said a friend or relative was responsible.[1]

Another study reported by Gary McIntosh and Win Arn showed that a year after joining a local church, people who remained active had made an average of seven friends, while those who where no longer active had made an average of only two friends.[2]

Results from such studies as these should impact the way we think about why we participate in a local church. Most of us participate in a faith community to be with friends!

How might you offer yourself as a volunteer to build strong relationships in your church or community? How might you lead in befriending people? Extroverts easily make their own friends, but many more introverted types quietly wait to be befriended. Are you gifted to meet this hunger for relationships?

People hunger for heroes–"...to the breaking of bread...with glad, sincere hearts, praising God..."

We admire the firefighter who rescues a child from a burning house, or the relief aid worker who puts her own health at risk to save others in a refuge camp. We celebrate the heroic, and we praise their selfless courage.

When the early Church "broke bread" together they remembered the shattering of Christ's body through Roman crucifixion. This one-of-a-kind, voluntary, sacrificial death of an innocent man, God's only Son, brought redemption to the world. Centuries have passed and the church has never stopped celebrating and honoring Jesus, the hero who put himself in harms way to save our lives.

How might you help people experience God's passionate, rescuing love for humanity? Are you an artist? A musician? A story-teller? How might you offer yourself as a volunteer to help people express gratitude for God's great love & mercy? In what way are you leading people in a fallen world to encounter Jesus' heroic act of redemption?

People hunger to connect with God–"…and to prayer."

Despite the brief, historically speaking, Modernist era where science attempted to eliminate the notion of "god" and most things supernatural, people have persistently longed for a connection with the spirit world. Legends, myths, and religions of all stripes describe the pursuit of communion with a god or gods, even if the legend describes these dieties as fickle, unreliable or malicious.

One Sunday, a friend, Diana, ventured into a Christian worship service at one of the large churches in our region, and she reported back to me. Her conclusion was mixed, "It was friendly, but I expected to meet God." She had met nice people, but she wanted more. In the midst of the polished music and programming, she was looking for Someone.

Prayer can be defined simply as "conversation with God." How might you serve others by a devotion to prayer (conversing with God) about the needs around you? How could you bring petitions to God regarding your neighborhood or city? Can you bathe your neighborhood or city with prayer as you walk or jog past homes and businesses? How can you help meet this human hunger for connection with God?

People hunger for meaningful service–"...they gave as anyone had need."

Most people want to do good in the world, something that will improve their community. Many want to make a difference in other's lives, especially when basic needs are unmet. People typically will help a friend clean up after severe storm damage.

But sometimes this deep desire to ease others' suffering goes beyond helping a neighbor through a rainy day. Some people abandon personal comfort in sustained sacrificial ways to bring good to others. They will deny personal pleasures, even empoverish themselves to care for others.

Starting around the year 1850, the Student Volunteer Movement sent nearly ten thousand mission workers to difficult areas of the world, often at great personal sacrifice. Many early young SVM workers went to areas with endemic tropical diseases, and they left with belongings packed in a coffin, fully aware that eighty percent of them would die within two years.

What desire do you have to bring comfort to others? How might you offer yourself as a volunteer to provide for unmet physical needs of food, shelter and health?

Your Contribution

In which of these Acts 2 areas do you experience the most passion and satisfaction? You may already serve as a leader and thus you will easily be able to identify where you are most typically motivated to pursue. Do you find yourself leading in one or more of these functions? In which of these have people asked you to take charge?

Or, you may not hold a recognized formal leadership title. However, when you do take initiative privately behind the scenes it will likely be in one of these functions. Can you identify which one? Consider these activity examples within the five functions.

Apostles teaching – Biblical instruction, mentoring, modeling, bringing sound wisdom to people who are looking for reliable information.

Fellowship – relationship building, counseling, coaching, encouragement, hospitality, connecting people in relationships.

Breaking of bread – worship, the arts, music, that honor Christ's heroic sacrificial love and help people see and feel God's redemptive work.

Prayer – Intercession, prayer walks, regular fasting and prayer, healing rooms, sermon response ministry, helping people to personally encountering God.

Sharing of goods – charity administration, construction, poverty relief, social justice, financial counseling, helping to provide the essentials of food, shelter, and health.

POST-CAREER DESIGN QUESTIONS

In what circumstances do you most typically function as a leader? List tasks in which you have led others:

From among the functions listed in this chapter, I lead or take initiative most often in the following:

During retirement, I would like to offer to help or volunteer in the following way within this ministry area:

CHAPTER EIGHT

My Creativity – What Can I Make?

*A*ccording to Scripture, the Living God created humanity "in his image." (Genesis 1:26-27) In doing so, God shared some of his capacity with our species, such as the ability to love, to have relationship, to communicate, and to be fruitful. The rapid-fire Genesis creation account slows down to give more detail of how humans were created, specifically describing how God took elements of the earth and formed human life. (Genesis 2:7)

It seems that our Creator God was delighted to endow humans with this creative, restless impulse to invent new things out of raw material. The wheel, the arrow, the pottery, the brass chalice, the steam train, the oil painting, the violin and the microchip all were invented from this creative attribute in humans, a reflection of the Grand Creator.

> *It seems that our Creator God was delighted to endow humans with this creative, restless impulse to invent new things out of raw material.*

The Boomer generation has certainly been apt to create. According to the Ewing Marion Kauffman Foundation, "Since 1996, Americans between the ages of 55 and 64 have had a higher rate of entrepreneurial activity than those aged 20-34. With many in this age bracket reaching retirement, but still wanting to work, entrepreneurship is an increasingly popular choice."[1] Some Boomers have thanked their Creator God for the gift of this inventive ability, many have not.

You may not have started a business. You may not hold a patent or consider yourself anywhere near being the inventive type. But, the fact is, nearly everyone creates *something*. You may have designed a quilt, or fashioned a new bowl in your wood working shop, or landscaped a new flowerbed. You may have experimented with a new combination of food in your kitchen, and you created a new recipe. Or maybe you have set up your easel and captured a sunset with acrylic paints. Teachers, you've created hundreds of lesson plans, or possibly written new curriculum. A spaceship it might not be, but likely you've created something.

Starting New Community Enterprises

In some cases where your local church does not have a calling or a capacity to operate a ministry in an area of your interest, or a specialized non-profit ministry doesn't exist for that need, God may call you to start-up a new effort. Michelle, a retired school executive, said, "Look, I have been a self-starter all my life, and retirement does not change that." She intends to keep on starting new ventures.

To take on the the significant leadership demands of such new community ministries wise congregations carefully expand their infrastructure. They know that they must preserve their primary function of discipling and nurturing people as followers of Christ, and so they know they must design additional structures to supervise and empower new innovative ministry. The early Church did just that when Greek widows were being neglected by food distribution. (see Acts 7) Church leaders expanded the leadership base so that ministry could expand without distracting existing leaders from their current work.

The local church is also wise to recognize that it does not need to control everything. Effectiveness can be released by forming new ministry development corporations, distinct from congregations, to operate programs in the community. This frees the local congregation to disciple people while freeing other leaders to provide leadership in fields requiring their expertise. For decades, John M. Perkins has been an effective practitioner of this model of community ministry development.[2]

Since the local church does not need to govern or control every ministry organization, it can collaborate side by side with non-profit ministries, foundations, and market place businesses. These all can honor one another and get more things accomplished.

Starting a New Business

While many Baby Boomers are retiring from day to day employment, others are reinventing themselves as new business owners. Active, healthy Boomers may find that retirement is actually a time to try working for themselves, putting their years of accumulated experience to good use.

The availability of starting an online business, or *e-commerce*, has created new opportunities to create a small enterprise. Many Boomers are tech savvy and welcome learning the computer skills needed for e-commerce. Nate, a former pastor, prepared for his future by developing his on-line pond equipment storefront, Practical Garden Ponds. Nate is using his extensive experience in designing, installing and maintaining garden ponds to create something that will add to his retirement financial revenue.

Kevin, also a pastor, has been turning high quality wood products on his lathe for years as a satisfying hobby. Recently, Kevin began taking his well-crafted bowls to art shows to sell, and to his surprise, he is winning "best of show" awards. So he formed a modest business to match his craftsmanship passion with a means to fund his post-career years.

Intergenerational Collaboration

Many dream of one day working for themselves. However, it can be overwhelming to make the leap from employee to boss, from practicing a specific trade to launching a new self-employed business. Not only must you produce the product you enjoy creating, but now as a business owner you add responsibility for marketing, financial management, shipping, and customer service follow-up.

Wonderful opportunities await for Boomers to team with a younger generation to start a new business.

An alternative to the solo venture is to combine forces with others. Wonderful opportunities await for Boomers to team with a younger generation to start a new business. The downtown gourmet coffee shop venture that Carol and I joined included two couples in their twenties and two of us in the Boomer generation. The younger partners provided the Prince Street Café with energy and innovation, and we older ones provided capital funding and other resources. For five years we worked together in an LLC, successfully reaching the point where one of our Partners and full-time Manager was ready to take over the business.

Mobilizing Your Professional Network

You may know others within your work profession that are eager to use their skills in a new venture. A group of construction workers might band together to form a home repair ministry, or auto mechanics might team together to provide simple repair service.

Jack McConnell was the son of a generous Methodist minister and habits of giving to others were instilled during his childhood. Having retired from a career as a pediatrician and then a corporate executive for Johnson and Johnson, McConnell expected to finish his days on the golf green and the deck overlooking the water at his Hilton Head gated community.

However, the contrast between the haves who lived in splendor and the have-nots—one third of the island's population—who lived outside the walls in squalor troubled McConnell. Restlessness for a more fulfilling retirement led McConnell to consider how he could bring together the many retired physicians and dentists and the working poor who needed medical assistance. So McConnell started a free clinic staffed by volunteer doctors, nurses and dentists, which eventually became the Volunteers in Medicine. McConnell persisted through resistance from physicians who feared competition, through legislation for medical licensure and malpractice insurance, and funding grants for equipment.

Five years after he conceived the idea the clinic was engaging 44 retired physicians, 64 nurses, 3 dentists, and 128 volunteers who served 6,000 patients a year with an annual budget of under a half million dollars. The clinic's mission statement states, "May we have eyes to see those rendered invisible and excluded, open arms and hearts to reach out and include them, healing hands to touch their lives with love, and in the process heal ourselves."[3]

Help a New Church Plant

A wave of new churches is being founded in many cities by twenty and thirty year-olds, in some cases by Boomers' grandchildren. These young leaders have zeal, passion and fresh ideas to engage the culture, and they crave the wisdom of humble, patient, visionary older adults to advise them. I coach church planters, and I consistently hear the wish: "Where could we find a few older adults who would join our faith community, willingly serve with us and help get our infrastructure in place?"

If the local church family where you participate is thinking of a creative new church plant or worship satellite, prayerfully consider how your skills might be useful. If there is no current planting initiative from your home congregation, your pastor may know of a church plant where you could be sent to help.

There are countless ways Boomers could fill crucial service roles in fledgling new church start-ups. Young generation church planters dream of creative Boomers who would dare join their cause. You might be a seasoned drummer to join a worship team, or a homeowner who can manage a new site rental facility, or a parent or teacher who can provide childcare. If you have managed your own finances, mortgage, taxes, and utility bills you could serve on a finance team or provide simple bookkeeping services.

Young generation church planters dream of creative Boomers who would dare join their cause.

One way Carol and I help young church plants is by offering to be a host home for midweek small groups. Younger leaders who live in small apartment flats are blessed by older adults who share their larger family-sized homes for hosting parties, Bible studies, and training events. Our current home is a central venue for a church plant in our city; we simply make the coffee and set up extra chairs in the living room.

Some people think that only "evangelist" types join new church plants. On the contrary, all kinds of practical skills are needed for both public tasks and quiet behind the scenes tasks. Both introverts and extroverts are essential for fullness and sustainability in a new mission.

So whether it is a church plant, a new business, or just a new way to make a task more efficient behind the scenes, consider how you can activate the *creative attribute* that our Creator has placed in every human.

POST-CAREER DESIGN QUESTIONS

List crafts, products, or items you have made in the past. What are you especially talented at making?

From the above inventory, pick several and list ways you might use this creative skill in a greater way for service to others or for supplemental income.

List a specific skill you might offer to a start-up team for a church plant or ministry?

List people that you might want to talk to about a team effort to create a new business or ministry. (See **Appendix E** for a guide to writing a new ministry or service proposal.)

CHAPTER NINE

My Schedule –
How Much Time Do I have?

*T*he traditional view of retirement paints a picture of a permanent vacation with complete freedom of time. According to a study of time-diaries by the University of Maryland's Survey Research Center, retirement frees up an average of 25 hours per week for men and 18 hours per week for women.[1]

Our culture can negatively suggest that one's career was a time thief, holding us hostage from enjoying life. You might hear a 65-year-old say, "I've done my time" as if work had been a prison sentence. For some, retirement is a welcome time to rest and relax, while others experience a terrifying sense of lostness. "Now that I have all this time on my hands, what do I do?" Many people spend considerable energy planning their finances for their post-employment years, but not on how they will fill the long hours. An otherwise happily married couple might experience new stress because a depressed, retired spouse is wandering aimlessly around the home with nothing to do.

"Free" Time

The Biblical vision of time is that every hour is significant. Paul the Apostle writes to a young leader named Titus, "I want you to give special emphasis to these matters, so that those who believe in God may be concerned with *giving their time to doing good deeds*, which are good and useful for everyone." (Titus 3:8 GNB, italics added) Paul adds, "Our people must learn to *spend their time doing good*, in order to provide for real needs; they should not live useless lives." (Titus 3:14 GNB, italics added)

In his letter to the Galatian church, Paul strongly encourages followers of Jesus to be free from external rituals to earn salvation. He writes, "Do not use your freedom to indulge the sinful nature, rather serve one another in love." (Galatians 5:13). This same principle could be applied to any kind of new freedom, including freedom from the demands of employment. In retirement with no boss to please or clock to punch one might be tempted to think, "I can finally focus on me and my pleasure. Paul might challenge the post-career Boomer in a similar way, "Don't use *your new free time* to indulge in selfishness, but use it to serve one another in love!"

Amy Hanson suggests that a new generation of older adults are beginning to approach life in a more *cyclical* way rather than the old *linear* pattern. She quotes gerontologist Robert Butler who suggests that our lives should not be segmented into three linear compartments of education (youthful years), work (adult years) and concluding with retirement (older years.) Rather, Butler says, "Would it not be better served by replacing the three tight compartments of education, work and retirement that evolved in modern times with an interweaving of all three throughout life...?"[2]

Butler's vision is that of a cyclical repeating rhythm of learning, then work, then rest, and then reengagement in learning and labor in fresh ways, followed by more rest. A century ago to "retire" meant to go to bed for the night, fully expecting to reengage in labor the next day. To "retire" daily allows for learning, working, then resting during both younger years and during older years.

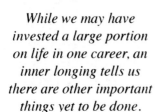

While we may have invested a large portion on life in one career, an inner longing tells us there are other important things yet to be done.

A by-product of aging is a deeper appreciation for the significance of each day. Retirement puts the brakes on the careening pace of vocational and professional careers and allows us to awaken to the fact that life is short. While we may have invested a large portion on life in one career, an inner longing tells us there are other important things yet to be done.

Many post-career Boomers are investing quality time with grandchildren, not only supplying them with more toys, but teaching them how to fish, or to ride a bike, or sew a scarf. This is not only an opportunity to pass on skills and wisdom, but to be a spiritual mentor. Grandchildren may have questions that they reserve for Grandpa and Grandma, and they will listen to your stories of faith in Christ through the thick and thin of life.

Some older Boomers are becoming *foster grandparents*. They help children learn to read and provide one-on-one tutoring for other educational needs. They may mentor a troubled teenager or a young mother. Foster grandparents may provide care for premature infants or children with disabilities, or help children who have been abused or neglected.

Mainline churches have partnered with the foster grandparent program of Senior Corps within the Corporation for National and Community Service (CNCS).[3] In some communities, churches have organized their own program, such as in Spring Hill, Kansas where the Paola Association for Church Action places older adults in the elementary school to interact with students and to assist the teachers.[4]

Of course, Boomers do not need a formal agency to offer practical life skills to a younger person. All it takes is an evening to prepare a meal with a teen learner, or a Saturday morning to show someone how to change the oil in the car. Ask a teen, "What would you like to learn to do?" and see what adventures emerge.

Enhanced Sibling Relationships

Other significant hours can be invested with siblings. While demanding careers with tough schedules kept sibling connections limited to annual holiday dinners, post-career Boomers now have the opportunity to reconnect with each other in a more regular way. I know of siblings who drive several hours to a centrally located city to enjoy a monthly lunch together.

While helping to serve the Christmas dinner to homeless persons in our city of Lancaster at the Water Street Ministries one year, we met a set of four older adult siblings who arrived to help serve for the day. Gathering from several states, these four couples rotate locations each year. The hosting sibling couple arranges for the group to serve at a rescue mission in his or her hometown, and they spend the holiday serving the poor together.

You may have opportunities to provide emotional or spiritual support within your immediate or extended family, and now you can give attention to needs that may have been pushed aside because of your previous work demands. You now have the time to listen to faith struggles, to explore questions about faith, or to read a book together.

Creating Space in Your Life

Lloyd, a church leader thinking ahead to his future retirement, told me, "I will need to create space in my life for the younger generation." When I asked him what that looked like, Lloyd explained, "That means more listening, more conversations. It means respect, not to be quick to criticize and judge, it means being there physically with an open mind in a relational way to create opportunity to share perspective and to impart values." Lloyd imagines often sitting in a coffee shop chatting with people, communicating hope, and helping someone find a sense of direction. When I asked him if he will take up golf, he smiled, "There is nothing on my white board for leisure."

One theme I heard echoed among many people I interviewed for this book was the desire to spend more time with people who are significant to them. Time spent with children or grandchildren. Time invested mentoring young leaders in unhurried coaching conversations. Time teaching people practical skills that will lift them from a cycle of poverty or failure.

Creating space for others requires not only openness of heart and spirit to listen to another's journey, but actual presence just sitting with a person. For many, reaching retirement age will mean a reduction of work hours per week, hours that become available to create this new "people space." For those who make a complete transition from all employment the newly available forty hours each week becomes a massive asset to steward. Will these new discretionary hours mean more free time for recreation, or free time to volunteer in a service ministry? Or for helping the poor? Or for helping reduce the church budget through non-salaried volunteer staff work?

How will you spend your time after you no longer need to record billable hours or punch the time clock? How might you establish new rhythms of learning, work, and rest?

POST-CAREER DESIGN QUESTIONS

List hours during your week that you expect will become available in your next phase of retirement, or "slow down":

List the primary places, people, or pursuits where you will allocate those hours:

CHAPTER TEN

My Health – What Physical Abilities Do I have?

*A*sk someone what they fear most about getting older and you'll hear concern about losing memory, hearing, or the capacity to do work. Many Boomers are caring for their elderly parents and they see the toll that aging can take on the body and mind. Many healthy Boomers wonder how long their good health will be sustained. There are no guarranties; aging can bring surprising illnesses.

In agrarian times, people worked until they were no longer physically able, whatever age that might be. German chancellor Otto Von Bismark may be credited with inventing "retirement" in 1883 with his scheme to resolve the under-employment of his country's younger generation. He declared that he would pay a pension to Germans over 70 who would no longer work. Bismark's shrewd policy came at a point in history when few people lived beyond age 65, and he knew it. (Germany lowered the retirement age from 70 to 65 in 1916). Likewise, in 1935 when President Franklin D. Roosevelt launched Social Security and proposed that retirement begin at age 65, the average American only lived to age 62.

Today we are living decades longer. In 1900 the average American life span was 46. Today it is 79.[1] A typical 65 year old American woman expects to live for another twenty years or more; an American male at least another fifteen years. Comedian George Burns, who lived past his 100th birthday, said, "Retirement at 65 is ridiculous. When I was 65 I still had pimples." With Americans living longer it is not unusual to have four generations all active in one local church.

Neither Young nor Old

The season of life between 50 and 75 is referred to by some demographers as "neither young nor old." Now that I am in my late fifties I can vouch that it is indeed a peculiar season of life. A few years ago I spoke at a post-high weekend retreat. The young adults politely asked if they could get me anything, as if this old guy might break a bone if I moved too fast. With eight grandchildren, I felt ancient next to them. A short time later I had the privilege to speak at Sunday worship with a group of 85+ year-old wheelchair-bound seniors at a retirement community. The frail but smiling residents shook my hand, "I knew your grandfather. We threshed wheat together...!" I went from feeling elderly to feeling like a mere kid, neither young nor old!

When I turned fifty, an elderly man assured me, "When you're forty, you're in the old age of youth, but when you turn fifty, you're in the youth of old age." Most of us will have more healthy years after 65 than previous generations. But not everyone. Sometimes serious heath issues can significantly limit the physical ability to volunteer and serve.

This was the case for Betty, an enthusiastic follower of Jesus who began to lose her eyesight in her older years. Eventually macular degeneration reduced Betty's ability to read or recognize people. Everything was a blur. Betty had always been eager to pray, but now she dedicated much of her daily work to intercession for others. She would often tell me of her delight in conversing with God and sensing his presence. Betty would chuckle about her long 99-year-old life, amused that she still felt young. She reflected, "When I ask God why I'm alive, the only answer I hear is that there is more to pray about!"

Insight from Physical Adversity

Betty found meaning despite her physical limitations. Sometimes a person finds purposeful retirement activity directly related to conditions he of she might have faced. In their book, *Shaping a Life of Significance for Retirement*, Jack Hansen and Jerry Hass tell Barbara's story. An accomplished commuicator, Barbara's career required regular speaking engagements before large crowds. She also had a form of diabetes. Upon retirement, she took a role with a national organization to travel and speak to patient and medical groups on the treatment and control of diabetes. Barbara found this post-career work tremendously satisfying.[2]

Billy Sunday, the colorful baseball player turned evangelist in the early twentieth century, is to have said, "I'll keep beating the devil until my arms fall off, then I'll kick him until my feet fall off, and then I will bite him until my teeth fall out, and when my teeth fall out, I will gum him 'til I die!"

Amy Hansen describes Scott, a pharmaceutical rep, who encountered serious health challenges while in his fifties. He took his struggle to a small band of men at his church that prayed with him about finding new significance. Scott loved football, and so he started a Fellowship of Christian Athletes chapter in his home, twice a month hosting as many as seventy high school boys in his basement. Many of the boys did not have active fathers in their lives, and Scott became a father figure to them. Scott has introduced these youth to Jesus, and some, along with their parents, have responded to trust Him.[3]

The loss of physical capacity can actually provide an opportunity to experience new satisfaction in helping others. For example, an accomplished pianist, her hands becoming painfully cramped with arthritis, sells her beloved piano and donates the proceeds to a medical mission among refugees. Her new involvement in relief to the poor becomes music to her ears.

Exercise as Service

The loss of physical capacity can actually provide an opportunity to experience new satisfaction in helping others.

Most Boomers have had good healthcare throughout their lifetime. Many Boomers have taken advantage of the enormous options for healthy eating and recreational exercise. Jim, a tutoring specialist, looks forward this way, "I'm preparing my body to be involved in coaching when I retire." Bruce, a pastor, envisioned that he would "keep up with as much physical exercise as is good and I am capable of doing so as to prolong my independent living and to put off dependent living for as long as possible, anticipating that our life-spans generally are longer than previous generations."

Medical evidence leaves no doubt that regular exercise is crucial to reducing illness and increasing life span. Ordinary chores such as mowing the lawn, cleaning the house, raking leaves, working in a garden, or walking for the mail are important for maintaining health.

Why not exercise by serving others? You could walk around the mall or the golf course, or you could walk with your pastor through a troubled neighborhood to pray for the community. You could pick up trash in the neighborhood.

Some people find that they are healthier in their post-career life because of reduced stress and more sustainable work and exercise rhythms. You might find that you have more physical capacity after age 65 than you did when you were younger. If so, it would be a sad waste to squander that renewed energy on self-centered recreation rather than on things that matter.

A Youthful Mind

While modern medicine has made hip and knee replacements accessible for many, the fact remains that our aging bodies will lose their young vibrancy. The clock cannot be turned back. However, in Ephesians 4:23, Paul states that our minds can be "renewed," to be *made new again*. He is saying that God can transform our minds to be "youthful" again. It means that we can face the changes, losses and unfamiliar experiences of aging with a youthful mental posture that is full of hope, optimism and eagerness to learn. The old axiom "you are as young as you feel" might better be stated, "you are as young as you *think*." Regardless of how your body feels, your mind can run and skip playfully with youthful enthusiasm and courage.

No Useless Christians

Exodus 17:8-15 records an attack on Israel by the Amalekites. As the battle was engaged in a valley under young Joshua's leadership, Moses held up hands in intercession before God on a mountaintop above the raging battle. As the day wore on old man Moses became weary of this simple physical task, and two assistants helped to hold up his arms. Even feeble hands made a difference, and Joshua prevailed. Weak Moses was not useless.

Peter and John, two early followers of Jesus, had scant financial resources, and one day when approached by a man impoverished from a disability, they could offer no money. "We don't have silver or gold, but we have Jesus!" they offered. The man was healed. Poor Peter and John were not useless.

Later Herod, the tyrannical ruler of Palestine at the time, imprisoned Peter. Helpless against a cruel ruler who had the authority to execute people on whim, the church met at a house and prayed. God intervened with a miraculous jailbreak, and Peter's life was spared. (see Acts 12)

So regardless of physical capacity, or even ability to be physically present on the front lines of the action, there are no useless Christians. In the Human Resource Department of God's Kingdom there is no unemployment, no layoffs. There are no white collar or blue collar job classes, and no one is on disability leave. Jesus describes the generosity of God's kingdom in a story of a man's declaration when paying his workers, "Well done, good and faithful servant! You have been faithful with a few things; I will put you in charge of many things. Come and share your master's happiness!'" (Matthew 25:21) All workers from top to bottom get a heavenly bonus at the end, not just the CEO.

In the Human Resource Department of God's Kingdom there is no unemployment, no layoffs.

Worn, but Valuable

Recently I spoke to an over-85 age group, many of whom sat listening in wheelchairs and electric scooters. I took a crisp new $20 bill out of my wallet and asked the group, "How much is this piece of paper worth?"

Of course they answered correctly, "$20."

Then I produced a thin, stained, faded decades-old $20 bill. "And how much is this old piece of paper worth?"

They promptly answered, $20!"

"Are you sure?" I prodded, "It looks pretty well worn out to me. Are you sure it's not worth only $3?"

$20!!" an elderly man shot back.

From their grins I could tell they understood what I was attempting to communicate. What made that little piece of paper valuable was not its physical condition, but rather that it was minted in the image of the original plate. Though worn, it would still buy groceries because the United States Secretary of Treasury's name was on it. The only thing rending it useless would be if it stayed in the wallet. Likewise, what makes every person valuable is that God made us in his image. And when the name of Jesus Christ is written upon our lives, we become more than mere flesh and bones, but rather as Paul the Apostle vividly declared to the Ephesian church, we become "the temple of the Living God."

POST-CAREER DESIGN QUESTIONS

Rather than focus on your limitations, list what body parts still work well, the parts that are strong (hearing, eyesight, smile muscles, hands, vocal chords, etc.):

List ways these strengths might be used for God's purposes.

What health disciplines will you pursue in retirement in order to sustain active physical service?

List ways you could combine exercise and ministry to others.

PART III – Serving with Integrity

Jesus said, "Live in me.
Make your home in me just as I do in you.
In the same way that a branch can't bear grapes by itself
but only by being joined to the vine,
you can't bear fruit unless you are joined with me.

I am the Vine, you are the branches.
When you're joined with me and I with you,
the relation intimate and organic,
the harvest is sure to be abundant.
Separated, you can't produce a thing.

(John 15:4-5 MSG)

The following chapters are focused on your relationships with others as you find a new place of significance in your post career life. Prayerfully invite the Spirit of Jesus to help you have healthy relationships with those with whom you will serve.

If you have trusted Jesus as your Savior and your Master for life, then your primary relationship is with Christ. He is the source of life no matter what your career or post-career oocupation might be. His character in you and through you brings integrity to your work alongside other people.

CHAPTER ELEVEN

Letting Go to Start Anew

*H*opefully the previous assessment chapters of Part II catalyzed thoughts about what new activities you might engage in that will bring a new season of post-career meaning. And you might be thinking of a project or two that you might want to pursue.

Amy Hansen points out that there are two types of volunteerism: *formal volunteering,* that is, serving with an organization with an assignment of specific responsibilities, and *informal volunteering,* the ways that we help others in everyday life, such as moving furniture for a friend, mowing a neighbor's lawn, or making a meal for a new mother.[1]

Both types of volunteering are meaningful, and we recognize that not every form of service will come with a title or with public recognition. Simple daily acts of kindness can have as great an impact as serving in a recognized highly visible position in a nationally heralded non-profit ministry. We can feel great satisfaction from these *informal* labors, yet we tend to measure our worth by our engagement in *formal* positions.

> *Simple daily acts of kindness can have as great an impact as serving in a recognized highly visible position.*

This may be the most difficult part of entering post-career retirement, and thus we declare our "un-retirement." Moving from being a *professional employee* to becoming a *professional volunteer* involves more than a mere change of work schedule; it also requires an emotional transition.

Change vs. Transition

It has been observed that *change* is different than *transition*. Change is what happens on the outside of a person in the external circumstances, the environment, and the context. But *transition* happens within the person; it involves a new way of thinking, a new attitude, and new self-awareness. One might *change* from employed status to retired status, but that same person must face *transition* from a feeling of meaningful significance in the former work to finding new meaning in some new work.

Steve Covey coined his 90/10 principle: "10% of life is made up of what happens to you; 90% of life is decided by how you react."[2] One could say that *change* is the 10% and *transition* is the 90%. Transition is what happens inside us and inside those around us to the new external context.

Stages of Transition

In their book, *My Next Phase,* Eric Sunstrom, Randy Burnham, and Michael Burnham, suggest four stages of transition that occur any time a major change is undertaken.[3]

1. Relinquish – Ending former routines, disengaging from responsibilities, turning in your keys (your privilege and authority).

2. Recess – A pause long enough to rest, recharge, re-create before moving on.

3. Redefine – Actively identifying new pursuits and planning new activities.

4. Reengage – Entering new routines and habits that bring stability and fresh confidence.

The late Dr. David C. Pollock, who served with Families in Global Transition, Inc. and Houghton College, developed and taught a transition model that included five stages.[4]

The Engagement Phase
Our response...
> Commitment – Belonging, responsibility, a clear role

The community's response...
> Status – Reputation, position, influence

Emotions...
> Intimacy – The comfort of familiarity, joining community, team membership, concern for others

The Leaving Phase
Our response...
> Finishing – Loosening ties, disengaging, relinquishing role(s), forgiveness

The community's response...
> Celebration – Gratefulness, farewells to people and places, recognition for service

Emotions...
> Denial – Feeling rejected, resentment, sadness, guilt over unfinished work or vision

The Transition Phase
Our response...
> Chaos – Lack of structure, exaggerated problems, grief, loss, emotional instability, disrupted routines

The community's response...

Statuslessness – No relationships, ambiguity of role, knowledge not used, skills not needed

Emotions...

Anxiety – Isolation (pulling away), dissolution of ego, self-centeredness, anger, cynicism, panic

The Orientation Phase

Our response...

Learning – Observation, uncertainty of trust, awkward application, new routines, learning from mistakes

The community's response...

Introduction – Initiate relationships, search for teachers, listen to new people, risk taking

Emotions...

Vulnerability – Uncertainty, easily offended, ambivalence, fear, loneliness, "homesickness"

The Re-engagement Phase

Our response...

Commitment – Belonging, responsibility, a clear role

The community's response...

Status – Reputation, position, influence

Emotions...

Intimacy – The comfort of familiarity, joining community, team membership, concern for others

We must release the past in a healthy way in order to embrace the next phase of life.

Both models of transition describe an emotional and social process that requires time and effort to navigate change in a healthy way. There will be chaos. There will be a sense of loss and grief over separation from that which we loved. Understanding, accepting, and working through the awkwardness and stress of transition is the first major step toward reengaging in meaningful work. We must release the past in a healthy way in order to embrace the next phase of life..

All Jobs are Temp Jobs (in this life)

Every job is temporary. Every role and title granted to us is a trust for a season. Some of us have held many positions and titles, while for others a single position spanned an entire career. But these earthly jobs are never ours to keep. If we founded an organization, a business, or a church, and if our formative ideas were responsible for bringing something into being, most of us don't want those grand endeavors to die with us. We want what we birthed to outlive us. But for this longevity to occur it will require of us a willingness to let others continue the cause.

Pastor Don Sweeting demonstrated this to his congregation in a tangible way when he transitioned from the senior pastor role of a local church. Don had acquired a baseball, signed by himself and the two previous pastors before him. Years later, at his own transition, Don presented the baseball to the new pastor who would succeed him, inviting him to add his signature. Don reminded the new pastor that the ball belonged to the Manager, not the pitcher.

Don said, "We pastors are like Major League pitchers. One is the starter. Then comes the middle reliever. Then another. When our time is done, the manager comes to the mound and takes the ball from us and we leave the mound. He then gives the ball to the next pitcher." He added, "None of us is indispensable except Jesus, the Chief Shepherd. We have our innings to pitch, but we don't own the mound or the ball."[5]

Armed with this attitude, we offer ourselves for service without residual expectation of importance or special status. If we knock on the door of our pastor or the CEO of a ministry to present an idea for ministry in the next phase of our post-career life, we must submit to that leader's decision as to when we come into the game to pitch, if at all. He or she might ask us to try right field instead.

Humility

Navigating the emotional and social loss and chaos of transition requires great humility, and this is hard for many of us. Those "know-it-all" types repulse us, yet we are tempted toward our own arrogance without realizing it.

"I can handle this transition by myself – I don't need anyone's help."

"I know what to do, and I don't need any advice."

"I'm mature; I won't make mistakes like other people."

"My situation is unique; I should get special privilege."

"Because of my importance I need few adjustments."

The truth is, we Boomers will not be exempt from needing others to help with a post-career heart and mind transition. Retirement can be very stressful because so much changes – and *transitions* – all at once. That's why I hope the assessment tools in this book are shared and discussed within a supportive group setting where friends can invest in each other's lives.

And so, wise post-career Boomers will take a humble posture:

"I can't handle the transition alone – I'll need some help."

"This is new territory for me, and I could use advice."

"I've not been here before, and I'll likely make mistakes."

"I'll need to learn how to serve you."

"I'm ready to be a novice again!"

> *It is no sign of weakness to ask for help or to seek counsel, especially at crucial life-changing moments in life.*

It is no sign of weakness to ask for help or to seek counsel, especially at crucial life-changing moments in life. The writer of Proverbs reminds us several times, "The way of a fool seems right to him, but a wise man listens to advice." (12:15) "Pride only

120

breeds quarrels, but wisdom is found in those who take advice." (13:10) "Listen to advice and accept instruction, and in the end you will be wise. (19:20)

And while we loosen our grip on our past positions and titles, we should do just the opposite with our relationship with God – we should hold on even tighter! After all, it is our relationship with God through the work of Christ that will sustain us through the emotional upheaval of transition.

Holding Tighter to Faith

After age fifty we can become less resilient, especially to the unexpected. Our preferences lock in and nostalgia shapes our memories. It was "better" back then. We make decisions drawn from the past rather than seeking God. In older age we might even discover that we are increasingly less interested in God's advice.

And we will be tempted to think there is little left to learn. We may read Scripture more superficially, "It's the thousandth time I've read about Moses parting the waters, for goodness sake, I've heard it all before." We will be tempted to rely on existing knowledge rather than on adding to knowledge.

By age sixty-five, we have a truckload of experiences, full of both regrets and of pleasures. We may face new battles with fear, worry, and cynicism as youthful optimism fades. My wife, Carol, saw this in her grandmother who was so concerned about the evil of the early twentieth century century that she couldn't imagine bringing children into such a wicked world. Accordingly, Carol's father was an only child.

But history informs us that the world has always been full of both good and evil, righteousness and decadence, love and cruelty. What happens as we age is that we simply experience more of the world and we see it for what it really is. Many of us see more clearly the truth of our own weaknesses and capacity to sin. A ten-year-old may be naughty, but living sixty plus years provides ample opportunity to be sinful many, many times. Maturity includes the humble recognition of one's capacity for both good and sinfulness.

Ezekiel 18:21-32 records an argument God makes for both our personal responsibility for ongoing faithfulness and for His mercy and grace.

> If someone evil stops sinning and keeps my laws, if he does what is right and good, he will not die; he will certainly live. All his sins will be forgiven, and he will live, because he did what is right. "Do you think I enjoy seeing evil people die?" asks the Sovereign Lord. No, I would rather see them repent and live. But if a righteous person stops doing good and starts doing all the evil, disgusting things that evil people do, will he go on living? No! None of the good he did will be remembered. He will die because of his unfaithfulness and his sins.
>
> But you say, "What the Lord does isn't right." Listen to me, you Israelites. Do you think my way of doing things isn't right? It is your way that isn't right.
>
> When a righteous person stops doing good and starts doing evil and then dies, he dies because of the evil he has done. When someone evil stops sinning and does what is right and good, he saves his life. He realizes what he is doing and stops sinning, so he will certainly not die, but go on living. And you Israelites say, "What the Lord does isn't right." You think my way isn't right, do you? It is your way that isn't right.
>
> Now I, the Sovereign Lord, am telling you Israelites that I will judge each of you by what you have done. Turn away from all the evil you are doing, and don't let your sin destroy you. Give up all the evil you have been doing, and get yourselves new minds and hearts. Why do you Israelites want to die? "I do not want anyone to

die," says the Sovereign Lord. "Turn away from your sins and live."

In this text, God reminds us how interested he is in our current spiritual state, not just our past effort. If you abandon your spiritual life in later years, the good you did earlier in life loses its shine. But turning to God, even in later years, is a delight to God. The current vitality of your spiritual walk with God is crucial. God wants a relationship today, not merely a scrapbook of old photos when you and He were once friends.

> *God wants a relationship today, not merely a scrapbook of old photos when you and He were once friends.*

Disciplines to Stay Spiritually Vibrant

There are several disciplines that followers of Jesus can practice to sustain a fresh spiritual life through older years. And if you are just starting to follow Jesus, these practices will strengthen your new walk.

Practice Gratitude. Dr. George Vaillant, author of *Aging Well,* describes his findings after a study of 824 people from their teens into their 80s. He found that one of the foundations of successful aging was a capacity for gratitude.[6] Author John Beilson advises, "So, build your gratitude 'muscles' and nurture a continuing sense of wonder and excitement about the world and its endless beauty."[7]

We teach children to say "Thank you" for the many things done for them. "Thank you, mom/dad, for making dinner." And as grown ups, we learn to respond "You are welcome" for the things we provide others. We are the adult providers for many productive years, and people are rightfully grateful toward us.

But past age 65 you sense a change. We must relearn how

to say "thanks" as people increasingly begin to assist us. We begin the transition from often being the provider, "You're welcome, glad to help," to more frequently being the receiver, "Hey, thanks for helping me find my reading glasses!"

I particularly enjoyed my weekly visits to Abner in the skilled nursing care unit. At 99 years old Alzheimer's had taken its toll on Abner's memory. I would read Scripture to him, verses that once were familiar to this elderly former preacher. But now, without the benefit of memory, it was like hearing Scripture for the first time! When I read the well-known "For God so loved the world that he gave his one and only son..." Abner exclaimed, "Why, that's wonderful! Read that again!" Or, "The Lord is my Shepherd, I shall not want..." Abner would interrupt me with gratitude, "Wow, that's an important truth! Thanks for reading that one to me."

> Paul the Apostle explained to the Roman church,
> "You see, at just the right time, when we were still pow-erless, Christ died for the ungodly. Very rarely will anyone die for a righteous man, though for a good man someone might possibly dare to die. But God demon-strates his own love for us in this: While we were still sinners, Christ died for us. Since we have now been jus-tified by his blood, how much more shall we be saved from God's wrath through him! For if, when we were God's enemies, we were reconciled to him through the death of his Son, how much more, having been recon-ciled, shall we be saved through his life! Not only is this so, but we also rejoice in God through our Lord Jesus Christ, through whom we have now received reconcili-ation." (Romans 5:6-11)

Paul's words are full of gratefulness, a "wow, look at this" enthusiasm. As I age I hope that I never lose the "WOW" of knowing God, and the wow of Jesus the Messiah who surprised us as a suffering servant to cleanse us from sin!

Practice Reverse Mentoring. Lisa, CEO of a large non-profit ministry, looks forward to retirement this way, "I'd love to be involved in mentoring, and in the process of that – learning from the younger generation. I'd love to be involved in teams with multi-generations – learning from each generation's strengths in order to more effectively serve people." She is anticipating a posture of mutual learning, and being re-tooled by younger leaders. Reverse-mentoring is when a younger person empowers an older person.

Paul instructed Timothy "Do not rebuke an older man harshly, but exhort him as if he were your father." (1 Timothy 5:1a) Paul implies that younger people will have a positive influence on those who are older. The original word for "exhort" (Grk. parakaleo) can mean encourage, console and comfort, and also to admonish and instruct.

Now that I'm in my late fifties I am aware that an increasing number of young people are leading me and teaching me. The current U.S president is younger than I am. My doctor, my dentist, and my accountant are all younger. Our adult children now advise us, their parents, from the insights of their professional training.

For several years Carol and I were involved in a small gourmet coffee shop business. Even though our company leader was younger than our own grown children, we learned much from her.

The older I get the more tempted I am to solve problems with *past solutions* rather *than new creative discoveries*. But by allowing younger leaders to mentor me, I can gain new insights that may have eluded me for most of my life. Who of us has not said at one point, "I wish I would have known that years ago!"

Practice Humility. Practice self-righteousness, cynicism, judgmentalism, arrogance... and find yourself ignored, isolated, rejected. But practice humility, listening, learning... and find yourself respected, sought after.

Once a woman accused of adultery was brought to Jesus to test his compliance with the Mosaic Law. What would he do with this sinful woman caught in bed with a man not her husband? Stones in hand, the crowd was ready for the green light to literally execute judgment! The Gospel of John 8:7-11 records,

> When they kept on questioning him, [Jesus] straightened up and said to them, "If any one of you is without sin, let him be the first to throw a stone at her."
>
> Again he stooped down and wrote on the ground. At this, those who heard began to go away one at a time, *the older ones first*, until only Jesus was left, with the woman still standing there. Jesus straightened up and asked her, "Woman, where are they? Has no one condemned you?"
>
> "No one, sir," she said.
>
> "Then neither do I condemn you," Jesus declared. "Go now and leave your life of sin." (Italics added)

In this event, the "older ones" led the way in humility! They were the first to admit that they, too, were sinful. Unfortunately, the accusers missed the fact that bringing the woman to Jesus could transform her *from* a life of sin. Jesus replaced condemnation about the past with new resolve for the future. I can't help imagining that if one or two of those humbled stone throwers would have knelt at Jesus' feet, Jesus would have also looked into their eyes and declared, "I do not condemn you, either. Go and leave your life of sin, too."

Practice Resilience. Resilience is the capacity to be fruitful and enjoy God no matter what the circumstances.

For example, that means you can cultivate the ability to

worship regardless of external conditions, to find ways to bless people, regardless of convenience. It's easy to worship and serve in familiar settings or when it is in your comfort zone, but maturity includes the ability to be a joyful, faithful Christ follower *in the unfamiliar*.

In 1976 Ron Wayne, an electronics engineer, met two young men in their twenties, both named Steve. The three men formed a company; Wayne designed a logo for it, and wrote the manual for their first product. The three partners drafted an agreement that gave Wayne 10% stake as their "adult adviser."

But Wayne did not last long in the partnership. He stated that he felt the new enterprise would be successful, but added, "at the same time there would be significant bumps along the way and I couldn't risk it. I had already had a rather unfortunate business experience before. I was getting too old and those two were whirlwinds. It was like having a tiger by the tail and I couldn't keep up with these guys."[8]

Wayne decided he had had enough "flights of fancy" from his youthful partners and he bailed out, abdicating his adult-in-chief role. Worried that he was the only partner with assets creditors could seize, Wayne sold back his shares and rights for $2,300 leaving Steve Jobs and Steve Wozniak alone with their fledging Apple Computer experiment.

In its first year of operations, Apple's sales reached $174,000. In 1977 it grew to $2.7 million, in 1978 to $7.8 million, in 1980 to $117 million and by 1982 Apple sales topped a billion dollars. By September 2012, Apple was the world's largest publicly traded corporation with an estimated value of $626 billion.

Had Ron Wayne held on, his 10% stake would be worth a cool $63 billion today. Wayne remains an obscure figure, living a quiet lifestyle in a Nevada pre-fabricated home selling stamps and rare coins. Ironically, an original Apple contract, dated April 1st, 1976, and signed by Jobs, Wozniak and Wayne, brought a staggering $1.6 million at a 2011 auction, or roughly a thousand times the amount Wayne received to get out of his Apple contract.[9] Wayne's story is a dramatic tale of opportunity missed because of not being resilient in the ups and downs of unfamiliar territory.

Paul the Apostle was likely in his mid-fifties when he wrote from prison in Rome. He says, "I know what it is to be in need, and I know what it is to have plenty. I have learned the secret of being content in any and every situation, whether well fed or hungry, whether living in plenty or in want. I can do everything through him who gives me strength." (Philippians 4:12-13) *Any and every situation*—that's resilience!

To another group of believers Paul wrote, "Be wise in the way you act toward outsiders; make the most of every opportunity. Let your conversation be always full of grace, seasoned with salt, so that you may know how to answer everyone." (Colossians 4:5-6) Not just familiar or comfortable opportunities, but *every* opportunity.

Resilience – the capacity to keep going no matter how hard times get!

It is easy to spend energy telling a younger generation what to do, but far more effective to show them what to do.

Practice being an Example. It is easy to spend energy *telling* a younger generation what to do, but far more effective to *show* them what to do. By living a life of peace, fruitfulness, and vibrancy, others will be inspired to follow your example. Stories abound in Scripture about people who taught others by the demonstration of their life. (Italics added)

[Jehoash] did what was right in the eyes of the Lord... In everything he followed *the example* of his father Joash. (2 Kings 14:3)

Follow *my example*, as I follow the example of Christ. (1 Corinthians 11:1)

In everything *set them an example* by doing what is good. (Titus 2:7)

To this you were called, because Christ suffered for you, *leaving you an example*, that you should follow in his steps. (1 Peter 2:21)

Is your life so full of joy that people want to be like you? Is your service to others inspiring others to serve? Think of it, our heroes are most always older than us. Are you one of those older heroes? Heroes – those people that go into the burning building rather than merely telling others to do it. There is tremendous opportunity to live life in such a way that younger persons say, "That's who I want to be like!" Imagine being a person that is a pleasure to be with, a person of inspiration, a person whose actions and lifestyle others would want to imitate.

POST-CAREER DESIGN QUESTIONS

Transition occurs many times throughout life, including:

From Mom and Dad (home)	to First Grade (school)
From High School	to college
From college	to work place
From singlehood	to marriage
From coupleness	to children
From former community	to a new community
From former occupation	to a new occupation
From former position	to a new position
From childrearing	to empty nest
From career	to retirement
From family-size home	to down-sized home
From independent living	to skilled care

What feelings and adjustments did you experience during one or more of the typical transitions listed above?

CHAPTER TWELVE

Submission and Accountability

$\mathcal{B}$randon Hatmaker tells the story of an extremely successful businessman who was radically changed by his new job as a volunteer providing meals to the homeless in his city. His new position of distinction? Handing out tickets at the front of the line. They call him the "ticketman." Hatmaker recites from an email, "A few years of my own metamorphosis 'dude too busy to notice suffering' or 'dude too quick to judge who deserved help' to 'ticketman.' I am no longer 'dude who flies first-class to Sydney' or 'dude having a drink at the top of the J. W. Marriott in Hong Kong'; just 'ticketman.'"[1]

Larry, a church planter and global leader coach, says about his future retirement, "I am hoping that I will be able to continue to mentor and encourage a younger generation of Christian leaders who will lead when I am that age, without having the personal responsibility to lead that which I have helped to birth."

Larry's anticipation echoes many Boomers who once held leadership roles and are willing to give up the need to have a hand in every decision. As you offer yourself for volunteer service, don't expect a high level of authority, even if you once had such a position. It is time to let go of governing control; allow others to make decisions you once made.

This is harder than it sounds because younger leaders will inevitably make decisions contrary to your opinion or preference. Some former leaders will feel compelled to offer unsolicited advice to save the younger leader from perceived disaster. But in reality, the new leader may have a fresh perspective that, in the end, makes their decision better.

Retiring Boomers cannot expect a younger generation to have the same life experience and skill that a sixty-five year-old has accumulated over a lifetime. We Boomers must remember our own mistakes and the things we could learn only through adversity, prayer, and hands-on experience.

Be an Encourager

> *When someone knows that you recognize their sincere efforts and that you celebrate their wins, they will be much more likely to invite your corrections.*

Instead of taking on a role of corrective advice giver, be an encourager! You will be honored to the extent you appreciate others' skills, hard work, and wisdom. When someone knows that you recognize their sincere efforts and that you ce*lebra*te their wins, they will be much more likely to *invite yo*ur corrections. Practice a 10:1 ratio. Offer ten times more praise for a younger leader's efforts for every one correction you assert.

In my previous book, *Inspirit Revolution: The Art of Transformative Encouragement,* I addressed how to catalyze positive change through intentional and persistent encouragement. I outlined four basic ways we encourage people:

Recognition – acknowledgment of something excellent, however small or incremental, that a person has done. "You did a great job today!"

Empathy – offering a presence during difficulty that goes beyond words, but communicates, "I'm here beside you to walk with you through the storm."

Admonition – inviting a person to consider a better way, offering a way to life instead of destruction. "You can do better than that; you are worth more than that."

Prophetic – offering a word about growth, accomplishment or improvement that you see, but that the person does not yet see or accept that is possible. "I see great things ahead for you."

A reality of aging is that we who are older will be led by many people younger than us, in some cases two generations younger! We Boomers must establish in our spirit an attitude of grace and appreciation. If we view ourselves as sages and younger leaders as fools, we will damage relationships, and we shouldn't be surprised if they have little to do with us. Rather, invite the Holy Spirit's authority over your heart to remove any pride that would sabotage a potential remarkable retirement legacy simply because you disdained working "under" some young, greenhorn kid.

The work of the Levites in the Hebrew temple duties was described in detail, including instruction about transition.

> The Lord said to Moses, "From the age of twenty-five each Levite shall perform his duties in the Tent of my presence, and at the age of fifty he shall retire. After that, he may help his fellow Levites in performing their duties in the Tent, but he must not perform any service by himself. This is how you are to regulate the duties of the Levites." (Numbers 8:24-26 GNB)

Some have taken this prescription literally as a mandate for early retirement and disengagement from meaningful contribution. But that misses an important element in the instruction. After age fifty, the older Levites were to *help* the younger leaders *without exercising leadership*. In other words, the over-fifty aged Levite became a servant to a younger leader who was in charge.

In the Bronze and Iron Ages, the approximate era of this Levitical instruction, life expectancy was thought to be only about 35-40 years.[2] Thus, there would be few Levites who ever reached that age 60+ milestone. And if a person would in fact survive to age fifty, they would likely be more than ready to step aside and obey such a mandatory retirement from leadership.

Obtaining a New Assignment

First, be candid. When you meet with a pastor or organization leader, be transparent about what skill or resource ideas you have that led you to the present conversation. Describe the idea you have, and the ways you might serve. (See **Appendix E** for a proposal writing guide.)

Second, listen. After you've shared your thoughts about wanting to serve, listen for the leader's response and his or her additional ideas. Offering to "help" with an idea that is out of step with the church or organization's vision and mission is not really "helping" at all. For example, an interior decorator might offer to paint the sanctuary with purple stripes, or a salesman might offer to set up a bingo scheme to raise funds. A leader has the right to say no. Honor your pastor's discernment about how you might be useful. Respect an organization leader who explains that your idea may be beyond their mandate. The fact that you have passion for a service idea is not enough, the idea must be confirmed as from God for this place, context, time, and mission field. If your idea does not fit, ask if the pastor or leader knows of an organization or context where the idea might be a better fit.

Ask your leaders what the greatest needs are in the organization, and listen for matches with your skills, knowledge and capacity. For example, you might ask your pastor,

"What is one underdeveloped area in the church that concerns you?"

"What do you wish could be done if only there was personnel to do it?

"What do you see is a need in our community where the church could make a difference?

"What is an area of your work that you would gladly delegate so that you could focus more on your primary calling?

Third, welcome supervision. If you sign on as a volunteer or part-time helper, expect supervision over your work, and honor whoever is placed above you. If it is not already in place, ask for supervision!

Report honestly and regularly. This can be very difficult for some older leaders. They may relinquish a title, but continue to express opinions with such a projection of rightness that a younger person may feel foolish to do anything other than what the older leader has "suggested." Thus the retired leader is still leading by intimidation with a lack of humble respect. Rather, take joy in *serving* rather than *leading*. Don't coast on past experiences; learn from your youthful supervisor. Learn how to work side-by-side to discover new courses of action and solutions to problems.

In addition to simply being too proud to accept oversight, resistance to supervision may come from past wounds, such as working under someone who was overly controlling or constantly critical. Supervision may be perceived as a hindrance to progress rather than a help. However, supervision is intended to be a healthy relationship that helps you succeed. If you fear supervision, pursue an honest conversation with the person assigned to your oversight. Give your supervisor the opportunity to communicate his or her commitment to supervision's healthy benefits, which include:

- Troubleshooting: help in solving problems
- Support: encouragement when the going gets tough
- Accountability: protection from false accusation
- Assessment: celebration of wins, and correction so that more wins can occur
- Resources: provisions to carry out the work

One mistake a post-career retired volunteer can blunder into is the expectation that because of your former stature you can always "go to the top" with a question or an opinion. A former CEO might expect he or she has the right to walk into the new CEO's office at any time, jumping past a lower level immediate supervisor. However, if you have recently taken a new servant role it is a valuable part of your mid-level supervisor's growth to discuss your practical operational issues, concerns and conflicts with them. Allow your direct supervisor to take the issue to a higher authority level if warranted.

For example, Ken, a retired pastor, now serves with his wife, Daphne, in the toddler nursery at the Saturday evening worship service of their church. When he has an idea for improving the care of two-year-olds, he goes to the young woman responsible for the Toddler Ministry, not to the Pastor.

Your Teamwork Style

Organizations universally promote teams and teamwork among staff and volunteers. And most people want to be known as good team players. However, there are at least two significantly different paradigms of what a person might perceive teamwork to be, and this perception will impact how he or she functions. Leaders, staff and volunteers can avoid accusing one another of "not being a team player" by recognizing these different approaches.

At times we must leave the comfort zone of our own personal teamwork style to flow with the objectives of an organization. Sometimes life will require you to step out of your usual preferred paradigm, i.e., a *process person* at times must act decisively, or a *decisive person* will need to patiently wait and discuss more in a longer process. Yet each of us has a unique make-up that leads us to be more effective as a team player.

POST-CAREER DESIGN QUESTIONS

The teamwork exercise in **Appendix C** can help you identify your teamwork style.

My primary teamwork paradigm is: _____

What kind of assignment would I work best in, an independent role or one with a lot of collaboration with people?

If you were to take a volunteer role, describe what kind of healthy supervision you would expect, or what supervision you would ask for if none is already present.

CHAPTER THIRTEEN

Retiring from Retirement

Each generation will announce to the next
your wonderful and powerful deeds.
Psalm 145:4

*A*ging never ceases, and eventually this second-wind post-career season will end. It has been wryly observed that "none of us will make it out of human existence alive." The human mortality rate remains at 100%. At some point age 65 becomes 85. Or, if you've faithfully eaten your daily parsley sandwich, maybe you'll reach 100.

Within high work-ethic cultures, such as my own Swiss-German heritage, laboring on is considered the only right thing to do. It is both an obligation and a badge of honor. People say to each other,

"I'd rather wear out than rust out."

"Enter death on the run and slide into your coffin in a cloud of dust."

"You should only meet death when there is nothing left to do but die.'

This bravado echoes the noble character quality of diligence over sloth, of perseverance over capitulation. However, this "never stop" attitude can also be a denial of the truth about aging and its limitations. It may be a subtle arrogance, a refusal to admit one's expendability and a self-centered view that the world cannot go on without me. It also may be an utter lack of vision for the amazing impact that upcoming younger generations can have if we get out of their way.

Jesus, fully aware of his approaching departure from his earthly life, cast his vision to his disciples, "I am telling you the truth: those who believe in me will do what I do—yes, they will do even greater things, because I am going to the Father." (John 14:12, GNB) Jesus was not only confident that what he had started would continue, but that with the Spirit's help, the disciples would take God's mission on earth to new heights.

Overstaying Effectiveness

One need not look far to see painful experiences brought on by a person who refused to step aside after effectiveness had waned. There is the cautionary tale of an influential and once fruitful California mega-church that was reduced to bankruptcy because the elderly founder continued to control activities despite a diminishing capacity for sound judgment. Or another pastor who refused to stop preaching and kept his congregation in a constant state of high anxiety every time he entered the pulpit because of the fear he would have a seizure and collapse at any moment in front of them and their young children.

Original founders of organizations, businesses, or ministries are particularly vulnerable to over-staying past effectiveness. What they started represents a life passion and often years of blood, sweat and tears of investment. Founders, movers and shakers forged their success on their ability to never give up. They often pressed forward when others would have quit. Obstacles, setbacks and nay-sayers do not distract determined pioneers. Thus, the notion of stepping aside because of a little challenge like an older, slower body is unthinkable. Malcolm

Muggeridge once said, "Few men of action have been able to make a graceful exit at the appropriate time."

Recently a leader described a difficult encounter at an event where the founder, after recovering from two strokes, returned with an expectation of high involvement in the event. He was the founder, so the team could not say no. Unfortunately, it soon became evident that, likely as a result of the strokes, his capacity for impulse control, discretion and thought process had been greatly diminished. His public speaking offended many event participants. His wife was embarrassed, and team members struggled with how to honor him while protecting the integrity of the ministry the man had founded.

No founder would ever want to destroy a beloved ministry, yet honest self-awareness about limitations is not easy, especially when advanced aging has dulled perceptions and clear thinking. And so retiring from being "retired" is another crucial transition to navigate.

Invite Others to See What You Can't

Steve, an over-sixty aged pastor friend, has authorized the elders of his church to speak candidly when he is no longer effective. In a similar way, a father gave a letter to his sons where he invited them to tell him to abandon driving a car when they felt he was becoming unsafe behind the wheel; his instructions were that his sons return the letter when it was time to stop.

If you are a leader, consider writing a similar "tell me when its time to stop driving" letter to your board, elders, or other appropriate advising or governing body to promote a healthy exit from leadership. Such a letter can bring a fullness of both honor and integrity. (See **Appendix D** for a sample letter.)

Invite regular feedback from those with whom you serve and work, and give them freedom to help you know when your volunteer years have reached a point where your service is more burden than asset. Assure them of your friendship and that you won't take anything they say about your effectiveness as a personal rejection.

Small Can Also be Great

Be prepared for diminishing roles and more simple ways to contribute. Welcome limiting adjustments as the years progress and be willing to accept smaller roles. Greatness is not measured by the size of the crowd or the square footage of the office; even the smallest contribution is noted in heaven. Simply passing a Dixie cup is significant! Jesus told his disciples, "And if anyone gives even a cup of cold water to one of these little ones because he is my disciple, I tell you the truth, he will certainly not lose his reward" (Matthew 10:42).

Later, Jesus expanded on the greatness of small contributions when He told his disciples:

> Then the King will say to those on his right, "Come, you who are blessed by my Father; take your inheritance, the kingdom prepared for you since the creation of the world. For I was hungry and you gave me something to eat, I was thirsty and you gave me something to drink, I was a stranger and you invited me in, I needed clothes and you clothed me, I was sick and you looked after me, I was in prison and you came to visit me." Then the righteous will answer him, "Lord, when did we see you hungry and feed you, or thirsty and give you something to drink? When did we see you a stranger and invite you in, or needing clothes and clothe you? When did we see you sick or in prison and go to visit you?" The King will reply, "I tell you the truth, whatever you did for one of the least of these brothers of mine, you did for me" (Matthew 25:34-40).

The service Jesus described may not carry a title or public recognition, but Jesus made it clear that he takes even the most basic acts of kindness to people as a personal gift. Imagine if the President of the United States were working the audience rope line at a public event, and I was close enough for a handshake. And furthermore, imagine if the President paused, sniffling from allergies, and asked if I had a clean handkerchief. I would give mine without hesitation. This encounter would be a favorite story to repeat to my grandchildren, "And then the Chief Executive sneezed into my handkerchief!" I might even consider this brief act of help to be one of my most memorable moments. Why? Because I perceived this person I served to be extremely important!

Jesus wanted his listeners to regard the recipients of simple service as royalty, not just charity cases. He wanted them to value acts of kindness as if they were serving a king.

Two Life-long Tasks

There are two assignments you need never give up, no matter your age or physical capacity: encouragement and prayer.

Encouragement. In the previous chapter we reviewed ways to encourage, and these practices can be continued until your dying breath. Encouragement inspires a younger generation to do their best, to press on toward goals that you both share, to extend accomplishments far beyond what you were able to advance in your previous active career. Sometimes, when adversity in life has knocked the wind out of a person, encouragement becomes as crucial as the respiration of CPR, filling the discouraged person's spirit

Encouragement inspires a younger generation to do their best, to press on toward goals that you both share, to extend accomplishments far beyond what you were able to advance in your previous active career.

with the fresh life-giving air of hope. Younger people are especially inspired when an older person believes in them.

Paul the Apostle instructed the early Church to "encourage each other daily." If all you do in your post-career life is make a simple daily commitment to speak an encouraging word to at least one person, you'll change the atmosphere of your community!

Prayer. At ninety-nine years old, Betty spends hours each day in her small retirement home residence room praying for leaders and people that she has mentored. Betty no longer travels, and her physical world involves slow walks to the dining hall. But her spiritual influence is global. She prays for a doctor and his family in Albania, a holocaust victim ministry in Israel. She prays for car dealers, young mothers, schoolteachers and nursing staff. Most of all Betty prays for people to know the gift of God's grace through Christ.

No matter where you are, in a hidden room or on a hilltop, or how physically distant from the concern on your mind, Almighty God can hear and respond. Prayer does not require riches or perfect health; prayer can be the last thing you breathe when your earthly life ends.

A Secure Identity

Those who finish well with grace and contentment are those who have anchored their identity in Christ. They are sinners who know they have been rescued by His redemption. They were once strangers but are now made sons and daughters in His kingdom by His mercy and grace. All other status, fame, titles, positions, accomplishments remain secondary and brief blessings next to the eternal relationship with Christ Jesus. If you are a Boomer contemplating your journey into retirement, rest in your secure identity as a loved child of God.

If, however, after reflecting on your future, you sense a longing to know Christ, and are even painfully aware that you have never acknowledged God and His redemptive work, then now would be the right time to welcome God into your life.

Sinful self-rule separated all of us from the holy completeness and perfection of God. Paul the Apostle observed a timeless reality, "As it is written [centuries earlier in Psalm 14:1-3; 53:1-3; Ecclesiastes 7:20]: "There is no one righteous, not even one; there is no one who understands, no one who seeks God. All have turned away, they have together become worthless; there is no one who does good, not even one." (Romans 3:10-12) In short, all of us are inherently bent on following our careers, ambitions, and pleasures with little thanks to God for creating us and with little thought that God might have a grand purpose in mind for us.

But despite this ignorance, or worse, arrogance toward our Creator, God acted to bring us back into relationship with Him through the Christ, who took upon himself the suffering that was really our due. Scripture declares, "You see, at just the right time, when we were still powerless, Christ died for the ungodly. Very rarely will anyone die for a righteous man, though for a good man someone might possibly dare to die. But God demonstrates his own love for us in this: While we were still sinners, Christ died for us." (Romans 5:6-8)

So here's the profound transformation that many followers of Jesus have experienced. It starts with a prayer, an admission to God of sinful self-centeredness, a remorse for the brokeness we've produced in life, and a grateful acknowledgement that Jesus took the penalty for sin in our place. After having that honest conversation with God, something begins to happen deep inside that creates a

Regardless of how godless your life may have been up to this point, the fear and loss that comes with aging can be replaced with a settled identity as a child of God, loved and redeemed.

longing to have God be rightfully placed as Master of one's life journey. God hears your confession of fallenness and he kindles a desire to surrender to his loving, wise, sovereignty. You invite God, "Direct me, show me your will and purpose," and he responds by infusing you with an unfolding sense of grand purpose and vision.

Regardless of how godless your life may have been up to this point, the fear and loss that comes with aging can be replaced with a settled identity as a child of God, loved and redeemed. Confusion and uncertainty can be turned over to the Master Designer of your life. Taking up golf will never satisfy or provide peace and hope like taking up God.

EPILOGUE

In his final days on earth, Jesus has a conversation with Peter about how Peter's life would end, that it would involve suffering, but that it would bring glory to God. (John 21:21-22)

Pondering this scenario, Peter looks around and sees another disciple, John. "What about him?" Peter asks. Jesus responds, "If I want him to remain alive until I return, what is that to you? You must follow me."

In other words, God has a unique plan for my later years and for yours, and what he does with other people around us is His business, not ours. I am called to be faithful in the way he wants to glorify God uniquely through me. And you are called to be faithful in the way he wants to work uniquely through you. To paraphrase Jesus,

> "If I want Lynn, after years as a physician, to volunteer for the Red Cross until I return, what is that to you? You must follow me."

> "If I want Chris to tutor at-risk kids until I return, what is that to you? You must follow me."

"If I want Bill and Jane to travel in an RV and help repair small rural church buildings until I return, what is that to you? You must follow me."

Here's the bottom line, let Jesus carry out his plan in you and through you. Let him be your new personnel director in your post-career life. Let your un-retirement years bring as much glory as possible to God. By God's grace, his purposes might be advanced more than you ever experienced in any previous job! As a fellow Baby Boomer, let's you and I anticipate the amazing years that lie ahead with excitement, determination and hope.

POST-CAREER DESIGN QUESTIONS

What has God shown you through this study?

My collection of ideas for service as I read this book include:

The top activities I/we feel God may be asking me/us to pursue would be:

(See **Appendix E** for writing a proposal for a new idea.)

I am/we are going to share these thoughts for prayer and counsel with:

Children (and grandchildren) _____

Pastor _____

Small group_____

Close friends _____

Siblings _____

Other _____

CHAPTER NOTES

Introduction

1. Marc Freedman, *Prime Time* (New York: Public Affairs, 1999), p. 19
2. http://wayofwisdom.com.au/wp-content/uploads/2012/03/ Ambassador-Joseph-Dublin-Ireland.pdf, accessed 8/30/14

Part One: The Boomer Journey from Middle Age to Retirement

Chapter 1 Background: The Boomer Demographic Bulge

1. James Tryslow Adams, *The Epic of America* (2nd ed., Greenwood Press, 1931) pp. 404-405
2. Gary L. McIntosh, *One Church Four Generations* (Grand Rapids: Baker, 2002), p. 86
3. Gary A. Adams and Terry A. Beeh, *Retirement: Reasons, Processes, and Results* (New York: Springer, 2003), p. 70
4. http://realtormag.realtor.org/sales-and-marketing/feature/ article/1996/04/aging-baby-boomers-theyre-not-babies- anymore/, accessed 8/9/13
5. http://www.cfr.org/united-states/remedial-education-feder- al-education-policy/p30141/, accessed 07/23/2013)\
6. Stuart Murray, *Church After Christendom* (Portland; Paternoster Pub, 2005), in Stuart Murray, Church After

Christendom (Portland; Paternoster Pub, 2005), from http://www.anabaptistnetwork.com/endofchristendom

7. http://elderstore.blogspot.com/2012/03/baby-boomer-statistics.html/, accessed 07/04/13
8. http://www.pewhispanic.org/2008/02/11/us-population-projections-2005-2050/, accessed 07/23/2013)

Chapter 2 The New Look of Boomer Retirement

1. http://www.55places.com/blog/not-your-grandmas-retirement-evolution-retirement-trends/, accessed 07/024/13
2. Sara Lawrence-Lightfoot, *The Third Chapter* (New York: Sarah Crichton Books, 2009), p. 58
3. http://www.trilogylife.com/lifescape/, accessed 8/1/13
4. http://articles.washingtonpost.com/2013-08-09/local/41222111_1_boomers-generation-city-life/, accessed 9/8/2013
5. http://steepleviewlofts.com/about/, accessed 8/1/13
6. http://www.trilogylife.com/lifescape/, accessed 8/1/13
7. http://www.aarp.org/about-aarp/press-center/info-04-2008/aarp_services_and_focalyst_release_third_quarterly.html/, accessed 8/1/13
8. http://www.babyboomers.com/about_nabb/, accessed 8/13/13
9. Marc Freedman, *Prime Time* (New York: Public Affairs, 1999), pp. 224-225
10. Ibid., p, 235
11. Brandon Hatmaker, *Barefoot Church* (Grand Rapids: Zondervan, 2011), p. 94
12. http://wayofwisdom.com.au/wp-content/uploads/2012/03/Ambassador-Joseph-Dublin-Ireland.pdf, accessed 8/30/14
13. Amy Handson, *Baby Boomers and Beyond* (San Francisco: Jossey-Bass, 2000), p. 28
14. Timothy Keller, *Generous Justice* (New York: Riverhead books, 2010), p. 132.

Part Two: Your Personal Assets for Retirement

Chapter 3 My Calling – What is My Unique Life Purpose?

1. Frederick Beuchner, in Parket Palmer, *Let Your Life Speak* (San Francisco, Jossey-Bass, 2000), p.16)

Chapter 4 My Skills – What Can I Do?

1. http://www.bls.gov/news.release/archives/nlsoy_07252012. pdf/, accessed 8/2/13
2. http://volunteersinmedicine.org/about-us/history-and-mission/, accessed 8/2/13
3. Marc Freedman, *Prime Time*, p. 120
4. *How to Finish the Christian Life*, George Sweeting, and Donald Sweeting, p. 58
5. Sara Lawrence-Lightfoot, *The Third Chapter*, p. 108-110
6. https://sellorelse.ogilvy.com/2013/04/08/ceos-advice-third-chapter-of-your-career/, accessed 9/4/2023

Chapter 5 My Stuff – What Do I Own?

1. http://www.babyboomer-magazine.com/news/165/ARTICLE/1217/2012-04-18.html, accessed 07/23/13
2. http://www.electronicstakeback.com/wp-content/uploads/Facts_and_Figures_on_EWaste_and_Recycling.pdf, and http://www.ce.org/News/News-Releases/Press-Releases/2013-Press-Releases/Mobile-Devices-Lead-Electronics-Purchases,-Finds-C.aspx/, accessed 8/22/2013
3. http://www.55places.com/blog/baby-boomers-26-percent-of-population-40-percent-economy/, accessed 8/2/13
4. Gary L. McIntosh, *One Church, Four Generations*, pp. 92-93
5. http://www.edgeresearch.com/casestudies_files/Edge_Research_Next_Generation_of_American_Giving_white_paper.pdf, accessed 8/23/14

6. http://www.businesswire.com/news/home/20130808005815/en/Blackbaud-Study-Reveals-Boomers-Give-43-Percent, acessed 8/23/14

Chapter 6 My Insight – What Do I Know?

1. http://livefaithoutatwork.org/?page_id=71/, accessed 8/23/2013
2. R.Jack Hansen and Jerry P. Hass, *Shaping a Life of Significance for Retirement* (Nashville: Upper Room, 2010, p. 46
3. http://www.scientificamerican.com/podcast/episode.cfm?id=brain-exercise-benefits-at-any-age-13-07-17/, accessed 8/6/13
4. Geroge Barna and Mark Hatch, *Boiling Point: Monitoring Cultural Shifts in the 21st Century* (Ventura, Calif.: Regal Books, 2001), p. 42
5. Stuart Murray, *Church After Christendom* (Portland; Paternoster Pub, 2005), from http://www.anabaptistnetwork.com/endofchristendom

Chapter 7 My Initiative – When Do I Lead?

1. Win and Charles Arn, *The Master's Plan for Making Disciples* (Grand Rapids: Baker Books, 1998) pp. 45-46
2. Gary L. McIntosh, Charles Arn, *What Every Pastor Should Know* (Grand Rapids: Baker, 2013

Chapter 8 My Creativity – What Can I Make?

1. *As Baby Boomers Reach Retirement, Many Turn to Entrepreneurship as Next Adventure*, August 8, 2012 accessed 8/22/2013 in http://www.kauffman.org/newsroom/as-baby-boomers-reach-retirement-many-turn-to-entrepreneurship-as-next-adventure.aspx/

2. Timothy Keller, *Generous Justice*, p. 146. See John M. Perkins books on community development, such as Beyond Charity: The Call to Christian Community Development (1993) and Restoring At-Risk Communities: Doing It Together and Doing It Right (1996), *With Justice for All: A Strategy for Community Development* (2011)

3. Marc Freedman, *Prime Time,* pp. 127-130

Chapter 9 My Schedule – How Much Time Will I Have?

1. Marc Freedman, *Prime Time*, p. 17
2. Amy Handson, *Baby Boomers and Beyond*, p. 79
3. http://www.nationalservice.gov/programs/senior-corps/foster-grandparents/, and http://www.seniorcorps.org/rsvp/foster-grandparents/, accessed 8/21/2013
4. http://www.usd230.org/shes/studentsparents/volunteeropportunities/fostergrandparents/, accessed 8/21/2013

Chapter 10 My Health – What Physical Abilities Do I Have?

1. http://www.cdc.gov/nchs/fastats/lifexpec.htm, accessed 8/2/13
2. *Shaping a Life of Significance for Retirement*, p. 45
3. Amy Handson, *Baby Boomers and Beyond*, p. 136

Part Three: Serving with Integrity

Chapter 11 Letting Go to Start Anew

1. Amy Handson, *Baby Boomers and Beyond*, p. 142
2. As quoted in http://allisonswonderland.typepad.com/living_in_allisons_wonder/2009/04/the-9010-principle.html, accessed 9/11/2013

3. Eric Sundstrom, Randy Burnham and Michael Burnham, *My Next Phase* (New York: SpringBoard press, 2007), pp. 84-85

4. David C. Pollock and Van Ruth E. Reken, *Third Culture Kids: Growing Up Among Worlds* (Boston: Nicolas Brealey, 2001), pp.66ff. and http://cfs14.tistory.com/attach/16/tistory/2008/12/25/10/47/4952e63e84a39, accessed 8/2/2013

5. Donald W. Sweeting and George Sweeting, *How to Finish the Christian Life* (chicago: Moody, 2012), pp. 78-79

6. George Vaillant, *Aging Well* (New York: Little, Brown and Company, 2002), p. 305

7. Beilenson, John. *The Future Me Journal: Authoring the Second Half of Your Life (Guided Journals)*, (White Plains, NY: Peter Pauper Press, 2003) p. 21

8. http://www.telegraph.co.uk/technology/apple/7624539/US-pensioner-Ronald-Wayne-gave-up-15bn-slice-of-Apple.html/, accessed 8/2/13

9. http://www.engadget.com/2011/12/13/apples-founding-documents-pull-in-1-6-million-at-auction/, accessed 8/2/13

Chapter 12 Submission and Accountability

1. Brandon Hatmaker, *Barefoot Church*, p. 115

2. http://www.news-medical.net/health/Life-Expectancy-What-is-Life-Expectancy.aspx, accessed 8/2/13. Also, Milton Eng, *The Days of our Years: A Lexical Semantic Study of the Life Cycle is Biblical Israel* (New York: T & T Clark, 2011), p. 40. It should be noted that life-expectancy estimates are disputed by historians because high infant mortality can skew overall averages.

APPENDIX A

My Story of God's Grace

Tip 1. If you describe only *external experiences* (upbringing, economic situation, tragedies, etc.) and people may respond, "That's nice for you, but my life was different." Instead describe *internal experiences* (feelings such as disappointment, rejection, confusion, loneliness, etc.) and any person, no matter what race, age or culture, will say, "I know what you mean!"

Tip 2. People already know what brokenness is like; they want to know if Christ makes a difference. So, describing Christ's *impact* on your life becomes the "good news."

Chapter 1: Childhood

During my childhood my understanding of God was...

During this time I felt (i.e., afraid, happy, lonely, rejected, worried, confused, etc.)...

I encountered God/Christ through...

Chapter 2: Teen Years

As a teenager, my perception of myself was....

And my understanding of God was...

I felt.... when I experienced...

I encountered God/Christ through...

Chapters 2, 3, 4, etc.: Adult Years

I felt.... when I experienced...

I encountered God/Christ through...

A Scripture that helped me was ...

Surrender to Christ Chapter

Trusting Jesus Christ for my salvation became clear to me through (person, book, song, verse, etc.)...

Because of Christ, I experienced a change...

Where once I felt... now I feel...

Because of Jesus' work in my life, I am learning to...

While I still struggle, I've seen God help me...

APPENDIX B

Teamwork Paradigms

Leaders universally promote "teams" and aspire to "teamwork." However, there are at least two significantly different paradigms of what a person might perceive "teamwork" to be. Circle a number on the scale to indicate the most typical way you think and function (not what you think others want you to be.)

Division of Labor		Zone Sharing
I expect to work at a task without interference from others.	5 4 3 2 1 0 1 2 3 4 5	I expect others to be involved in the task I am working at.
I enjoy work where I am assigned a task that I alone must accomplish.	5 4 3 2 1 0 1 2 3 4 5	I enjoy work where others accomplish parts of my task.
I value the efficiency of letting one person get the job done.	5 4 3 2 1 0 1 2 3 4 5	I value the relationship of letting others have a piece of the action.
The important thing is the personal satisfaction of completing a task.	5 4 3 2 1 0 1 2 3 4 5	The important thing is the task completion, not who did it.
I find it very confusing when multiple people are responsible for the same task.	5 4 3 2 1 0 1 2 3 4 5	I find it energizing when role assignments are fluid and interchangeable.

I feel frustrated with people who step out of their assigned role.	5 4 3 2 1 0 1 2 3 4 5	I feel frustrated with people who refuse to step out of their assigned role.
I admire people who restrain themselves from doing things that are not their job.	5 4 3 2 1 0 1 2 3 4 5	It is frustrating when someone could do something and they don't because it's "not their job."
It is frustrating when people do things without permission.	5 4 3 2 1 0 1 2 3 4 5	I admire people who can "pitch in" without being told.
In our home, one spouse does all the cooking.	5 4 3 2 1 0 1 2 3 4 5	In our home, whoever gets home first starts making dinner.
One person in our family does all the grocery shopping; that way we never duplicate.	5 4 3 2 1 0 1 2 3 4 5	Whoever in our family is near a store picks up needed groceries, and sometimes we end up with duplicates.
I enjoy teams where each person has their own clearly defined sphere of work.	5 4 3 2 1 0 1 2 3 4 5	I enjoy teams where people share responsibilities jointly.
In our home, one person maintains and repairs things.	5 4 3 2 1 0 1 2 3 4 5	In our home, the entire household does maintenance tasks.
I feel valued and have a sense of meaning when I have a specific job task. When that task changes or is removed I feel a loss of value and meaning.	5 4 3 2 1 0 1 2 3 4 5	I feel valued and have a sense of meaning when many individuals are helping with a specific task. If that task is solely up to me I feel a loss of value and meaning
I find it irritating and disrespectful when someone openly opposes my leadership in a group.	5 4 3 2 1 0 1 2 3 4 5	I find it irritating and disrespectful when someone opposes my leadership but remains silent about it in a group.

I appreciate when others let me do my work without opposing me or intruding on my work.	5 4 3 2 1 0 1 2 3 4 5	I am energized by opposing ideas and interruptions in the middle of a task.
(If applicable) In parenting, one of us primarily carries out bathing, clothing and bedtime routines with our children.	5 4 3 2 1 0 1 2 3 4 5	(If applicable) In parenting, on any given day either one of us might be involved in bathing, clothing and bedtime child care routines.
I prefer meetings where people talk when it is their turn; I like to know where I am in "the batting order."	5 4 3 2 1 0 1 2 3 4 5	I prefer meetings where the unexpected happens; I like when others "butt in" with an idea.
If someone else assumes a task I thought I was supposed to do, I will back off completely and let them do it.	5 4 3 2 1 0 1 2 3 4 5	If someone else assumes a task I thought I was supposed to do, I will ask if they need my help in any way.
It bothers me when people do things outside of the planned order of events.	5 4 3 2 1 0 1 2 3 4 5	It bothers me when people don't feel free to do something outside of the planned order of events.

Total from left of zero _____ _____ Total from right of zero

159

Teamwork Paradigm Results

My primary teamwork paradigm is: _____

If already on a team:

In what ways is my teamwork style compatible with others with whom I work?

In what ways does this or has this clashed with others' practice of teamwork within my work environment?

If anticipating a new activity:

In what kind of assignment would I work best, a role requiring independence or one with a lot of interaction?

Teamwork Paradigm Descriptions

	Division of Labor	Zone Sharing
Biblical Example	Romans 15:20 "It has always been my ambition to preach the gospel where Christ was not known, so that I would not be building on someone else's foundation."	Mark 9:38-40 "Teacher," said John, "we saw a man driving out demons in your name and we told him to stop, because he was not one of us." "Do not stop him," Jesus said. "No one who does a miracle in my name can in the next moment say anything bad about me, for whoever is not against us is for us."
Corporate Model	An expert is hired or trained in one skill field or for one task on an assembly line.	Personnel is hired or trained for several jobs with workers shifting positions routinely., called "cross training" in some industries.
Metaphor	*(American) Baseball*–the batter is responsible to hit, run and score while the rest of the team watches from the dugout; they will not help him. The base coach gives advice from the boundaries of his "box."	*(International) Soccer*–several players attempt to score, and in the scuffle any one of 3-4 players might score. The ball is passed to the one who happens to be at the right place for a good shot.
Relationship with Other Workers	Passing work to another is "shirking responsibility" or "passing the buck." Sticking to one's job until it is completed is honored as responsible diligence.	Passing work to others is expected and trading is frequent; "assists" are honored. Sticking to a task *without* passing is dishonored as self-centered "hogging the ball."

Personal Identity	Feelings of value and a sense of meaning in life are connected to engagement in a specific job task. When that task changes or is removed, that individual feels an acute loss of value and meaning.	Feelings of value and a sense of meaning in life are connected to the overall goal being completed by many individuals. When a task is left solely to one person, that individual feels an acute loss of value and meaning.
Domestic Application	One spouse does all the cooking, cleaning, etc. and the other earns the money. One person does shopping; the other maintains the car.	Whoever gets home first starts dinner or the laundry. Whoever is near a store picks up what is needed. A washing machine was recently invented with a sensor not allowing the same person to operate it twice in a row.
Church Identity Application	In the Roman parish system, a priest is assigned to an area and boundaries are defined about what pastors can and can't do with a member of other congregations. Member loyalty is expected to only one organization, congregation or denomination at a time.	Leaders network in relationships, regional leaders collaborate and refer matters and members to one another. A believer may participate actively in several organizations, congregations or movements simultaneously.
Worship Application	Worship service is led in segments, where each person respects the other participants by waiting his/her turn to provide a distinct function.	Worship service is planned holistically, each person fully aware of the other leaders' agenda so as to enhance the other leaders' functions.
Cultural Background	The Industrial Age and its assembly lines created a culture of one-job roles; i.e., a worker installs fenders all day and never "meddles" with the windshield installer. The world war generation was schooled in chain of a command leadership of precise division of rank and role.	An agrarian and craftsman/ artisan culture meant that everyone on the team could do 80% of the tasks, i.e. the farmer or any of his sons could plow or feed cattle or repair machinery on any given day. The rapid-changing high tech age has trained millenials to expect ever-shifting roles.

APPENDIX C

"Stop Driving" Letter

Dear _____,

It has been my privilege to serve with you (in the position of_____) and I value your friendship and your commitment to our common vision and mission.

As I age I know that my capacity will change and thus my contribution to this organization may be diminished. My mental and emotional state may also begin to trick me into thinking that I am as vigorous and as effective as ever, but you may notice otherwise.

I invite you to be watchful of the things I can longer see or understand and to tell me with love and candidness when it is time to turn in my "driving keys" in my present role before I cause damage. Tell me honestly what areas are losing effectiveness, and I commit myself to honoring your insight. I entrust this discernment to you so that the things we love about our mutual work are not compromised and the work can continue to thrive.

Read this letter to me and remind me of these things:

- That God can and will carry on His purposes with other people, and His success does not depend solely on me.
- That I am a child of God because of my faith in Christ, not because of any role or title.

- That asking me to hand over responsibilities is an act of love, not an act of rejection.
- That God will show me what new assignment might be useful within my current stage of life.

Thank you for helping me to serve God's kingdom.

Sincerely,

APPENDIX D

Boomer Mobilization Form

Name_____ Date_____

Please give a brief description of your life calling.

What skills would you like to offer?

What training would you like to explore?

What other assets or resources would you like to offer?

Are you primarily a...

_____ People connector: I love interacting with people.
_____ Idea generator: I love to dream up new things.
_____ Vision communicator: I love to explain things to people.
_____ Detail organizer: I love to arrange things behind the scenes.

How many hours a week would you be available? On what days? What months or seasons are you available?

Check the type(s) of activity situations in which you would be available to serve:

_____ Episodic: Activity held annually or several times a year.
_____ Seasonal: Intense activity for a short period of weeks.
_____ Stationary: Activity always at the same place
_____ Mobile: Activity that requires travel to various locations.
_____ Year-round: Activity that has a regular ongoing routine.
_____ Substitute: Be on call to fill in as needed.

APPENDIX E

Ministry or Service Proposal

The following may be a template for composing a proposal for a new ministry or project.

Part 1 – *Introduction:* Include your name and your connection with the organization, church or ministry to which you are offering the proposal.

Part 2 – *Background:* Describe how you came to the idea and why it is or could be a strategic priority to be connected with this organization.

Part 3 – *Vision:* In a clear sentence or two explain what you hope to accomplish and what success will look like. We will know the idea/project has succeeded when the following occurs...

Part 4 – *Examples:* If available, describe places where this idea has been tried and what others have learned.

Part 5 – *Personnel:* List what skills and people are needed to implement the idea and where they will be found. Describe what your role will be.

Part 6 – *Finances:* Describe finances that are needed to support the idea and from where these funds could come.

Part 7 – *Timetable:* Describe when you hope the idea will be launched and for how long it will continue.

Other Books by Dave Witmer

Inspirit Revolution:
The Art of Transformational Encouragement
(Xulon Press)

"Rooted in the timeless wisdom of the Scriptures and grounded in practical experiences of daily life, *In-spirit Revolution* is among the few that is life-changing. I heartily recommend this book to all who seek to thrive rather than merely survive, and to influence their world by calling forth and cultivating all that is good."
— Don Riker, *Coach to business and church leaders*

In a pessimistic cynical world a revolution is needed in the human spirit of how we think and act to inspire each other to grow and flourish. Encouragement should never be anything less than provocative rebellion against the tyranny of a condemning world.

This book is for those of you who long to hear encouragement, and who want to perfect the art of genuine encouragement to others to make relationships work.

If you are weary of a negative world, and you hope that there is a better way inspire greatness, then this book will inspire you. The ancient biblical mandate to *"encourage one another daily"* calls for a deeply spiritual activity that must become a staple for life in the emerging culture of the new millennium.

CPSIA information can be obtained at www.ICGtesting.com
Printed in the USA
BVOW04s2211100215

387176BV00006B/13/P